'Selina Mills's defiant book is a thun[...] our sighted notions of blindness, a [...] cry for a revolution in our age-old perceptions of being blind that should be read by sighted people everywhere.'

WENDY MOORE, *Times Literary Supplement*

'Written with wit, warmth and razor-sharp insight, this book should be essential reading for anyone with an interest in blindness, history, society, culture and beyond.'

ANNA BONET, *The i* (Non-fiction Book of the Month)

'Informative, heartfelt ... This admirable book dispels myths around the condition.'

MARTIN CHILTON, *Independent*

'A much-needed and powerful examination of what it is to be blind.'

SIMON EVANS, *Choice*

'Spirited, irreverent ... *Life Unseen* offers an illuminating peek into one woman's world, and asks searching questions of us all in terms of the different ways in which we perceive our world. There are no glib answers because blindness, as *Life Unseen* demonstrates, is a subject riven with ambiguity and complexity. In this important and hugely enjoyable book, Mills clears away some of the myths and injustices that surround it.'

SUSAN FLOCKHART, *The Herald*

'Spirited . . . [A] powerful memoir-cum-manifesto.'

YSENDA MAXTONE GRAHAM,
The Spectator

'A powerful and erudite social history of blindness in the Western world interwoven with an extraordinarily moving but unsentimental account of her own gradual life-long descent into blindness.'

JULIA HAMILTON, *The Catholic Herald*

'It's an extraordinary account of blindness, the mythology that surrounds it, the fallacies and taboos connected to it, and the attitudes towards it throughout the ages. Written by an author who is herself blind, it's filled with fascinating information, practical insights and teaching moments about the nature of imagination, language and perception of our world.'

JOANNE HARRIS, *Guardian*

'Part history, part memoir, part manifesto, *Life Unseen* is smart, powerful and funny. Selina Mills is a word painter of rare originality, creating a picture of a world where sightlessness is neither black nor white but shades of being.'
AMANDA FOREMAN, author of *Georgiana, Duchess of Devonshire*

'Selina Mills de-mystifies blindness both in its material reality as well as its manifold superstitions. That she does this with wit and intelligence makes this a superb and memorable read.'
STEPHEN KUUSISTO, author of *Planet of the Blind*

'Selina Mills crafts a compelling narrative that illuminates and animates the story of a community that has always existed but has been relegated to the margins and the shadows. Mills takes readers along on her personal journey as she comes to terms with her own blindness with candor and warmth. She shares her fears, her irritation, her rage, and yes, her joy, as her contemporary story resonates with the lives of famous and lesser known blind writers, musicians, inventors and leaders from the past and present. This book will help to reform the image of blindness from a tragedy that must be overcome to simply another facet of human diversity.'
GEORGINA KLEEGE, author of *Sight Unseen*

'The metanarrative of blindness hangs over us all, invites us to identify as sighted or blind, and thus to follow numerous binary assumptions that pertain to everything from sexuality to epistemology. *Life Unseen* helps to disrupt the myths, tropes, and stereotypes of the metanarrative via the often under-rated power of memoire. As such, the book makes an important contribution to blindness studies.'
> DAVID BOLT, Professor of Disability Studies and Interdisciplinarity at Liverpool Hope University

'A beautiful, tender and inspiring book about seeing the world in a different way.'
> PETER FRANKOPAN, author of *The Earth Transformed* and *The Silk Roads*

LIFE UNSEEN

A Story of Blindness

Selina Mills

BLOOMSBURY ACADEMIC
LONDON • NEW YORK • OXFORD • NEW DELHI • SYDNEY

BLOOMSBURY ACADEMIC
Bloomsbury Publishing Plc
50 Bedford Square, London, WC1B 3DP, UK
1385 Broadway, New York, NY 10018, USA
29 Earlsfort Terrace, Dublin 2, Ireland

BLOOMSBURY, BLOOMSBURY ACADEMIC and the Diana logo are
trademarks of Bloomsbury Publishing Plc

First published in Great Britain 2023
Paperback edition published 2024

Copyright © Selina Mills, 2023

Selina Mills has asserted her right under the Copyright, Designs and Patents Act, 1988, to be identified as Author of this work.

For legal purposes the Acknowledgements on pp. 251–4 constitute
an extension of this copyright page.

Cover design by Graham Robert Ward
Cover image © Giovanni Coppola: jonnycoppola@gmail.com

All rights reserved. No part of this publication may be reproduced or transmitted in any form or by any means, electronic or mechanical, including photocopying, recording, or any information storage or retrieval system, without prior permission in writing from the publishers.

Bloomsbury Publishing Plc does not have any control over, or responsibility for, any third-party websites referred to or in this book. All internet addresses given in this book were correct at the time of going to press. The author and publisher regret any inconvenience caused if addresses have changed or sites have ceased to exist, but can accept no responsibility for any such changes.

A catalogue record for this book is available from the British Library.

Library of Congress Cataloging-in-Publication Data

Names: Mills, Selina (Journalist), author.
Title: Life unseen : a story of blindness / Selina Mills.
Description: London ; New York : Bloomsbury Academic, 2023. |
Includes bibliographical references and index.
Identifiers: LCCN 2023002762 (print) | LCCN 2023002763 (ebook) |
ISBN 9781848856905 (hardback) | ISBN 9781350349735 (epub) |
ISBN 9781350349728 (pdf) | ISBN 9781350349742
Subjects: LCSH: Blind–History. | Blind–Biography.
Classification: LCC HV1581 .M555 2023 (print) | LCC HV1581 (ebook) |
DDC 305.9/081–dc23/eng/20230510
LC record available at https://lccn.loc.gov/2023002762
LC ebook record available at https://lccn.loc.gov/2023002763

ISBN: HB: 978-1-8488-5690-5
PB: 978-1-3505-0721-0
ePDF: 978-1-3503-4972-8
eBook: 978-1-3503-4973-5

Typeset by RefineCatch Limited, Bungay, Suffolk
Printed and bound in Great Britain

To find out more about our authors and books visit www.bloomsbury.com
and sign up for our newsletters.

In memory of my father Robert Mills (1939–2019)
A giant amongst men and bears

CONTENTS

Prologue 1

1 Imagining it – Nandy and mythic heroes 19

2 Living with it – dark versus light 49

3 Faking it – false eyes, false sight, and the Devil 79

4 Fixing it – the lure of the cure 107

5 Learning it – education, education, education 141

6 Reading it – pure fiction 187

7 Inventing it – the advantages of blindness (and disadvantages of tech) 213

Conclusion   What is blindness anyway? 243

Acknowledgements 251
Bibliography 255
Index 267

Prologue

Close your eyes.

No seriously.

For one moment, put down this book, close your eyes and imagine you are blind.

Now take a deep breath and open them.

Most people in the sighted world think that what they have just experienced – that velvet, pinky darkness behind our lids – is blindness. Merely closing our eyes will give us a moment of awareness into what it is like not to be able to use our eyes at all. Blindness, we tell our sighted selves, is a state of darkness, blackness, obscurity, or at least murky fogginess. Indeed, any mention of the word 'blind' or 'blindness' comes with an elusive coat of mystery, intrigue and ultimately fear. Blindness is portrayed either as debilitating – blind people with their arms stretched out groping in the dark – or as creating passive and miserable souls, who must be grateful for what morsels the sighted world gives them.

In our far less damning and supposedly more liberal times, there is a clear legal definition of blindness (legally, blindness is defined as less than 20/200 vision in the better eye with glasses[1]) and we live in a world where we have white canes, assistive technology and well-trained guide dogs, not to mention vast strides in medical care. Yet we still think of blindness as tragic and frightening; a clinical condition to be diagnosed, fixed and ultimately triumphed over.

It's curious, isn't it?

---
[1] Blindness and vision impairment (who.int).

PROLOGUE

* * *

My own curiosity about the state of blindness comes from having, in 2002, begun to lose my own sight.

Apart from the rounds of doctors and tests and dealing with the prognosis, the idea of blindness seemed far removed from the sighted world I occupied – a tough City journalist at the *Daily Telegraph*. I have always had eyesight problems, and the sight I have had has been precarious. As my father was prone to say, I was born in a year for good Bordeaux, and blind in my right eye. The wonky working eye – which had all sorts of things that didn't work – allowed me to function with a bit of sight from birth, and I learnt to adapt. When I was asked, I explained it was as if Vaseline had been wiped across my one working eye, and that was the only world I knew. It was not a problem.

It was not until my early to mid-thirties that the world became a bit blurrier, and I started falling over the treads of stairs, not reading large adverts or the TV, and cutting my fingers with the kitchen knife. At first, I put such clumsiness down to fatigue as I was a busy journalist, being forever self-important. But finally, I realized I could no longer see the edges of pavements and the numbers on buses. Something was amiss in the seeing department.

Off I trundled to an ophthalmologist, who spied deeply into the back, the front and all around my eye and seemed somehow pleased. 'It's a post-anterior cataract,' he said, sitting back on his chair. 'It reminds me of Caithness crystal I bought my wife last year on a fishing trip up north to Sutherland.' I waited for the more medical view. He pondered. 'Yes, it's beautiful . . .' What this 'beautiful' growth would do for and to me was another affair, but as he signed me off years later as 'legally blind', I often wonder if he had any concept of how his charming manner belied the impact on my life. How did he imagine, now more blind than seeing, I would magically navigate the world? Know how to find my food on a plate? Even negotiate leaving the room without falling over the three chairs I counted when I entered? The silence over how to live a life with blindness was loud.

It took me some time to digest the news, and I was, as I imagine most of us would be, surprised to learn how little could be done. In fact, according to the World Health Organization, blindness is on the rise, with over a billion people with complete or severe vision loss worldwide, and 48 million with the visual acuity of less than 1/10 (legal blindness) – and that is only the people we know of. In Britain alone, over two million people are registered blind or severely sight impaired. In the United States, there are twelve million. Blindness is far more prevalent than you can imagine.[2]

More than anything, however, as I adjusted to my increasingly blurry world, I was astonished by the variety of ways people, both acquaintances and strangers, treated the news of my impending sight loss. Some of my friends saw it as a catastrophic calamity, worthy of pity, and I was rather surprised to hear heavy sighs on delivering the news. Others were desperate to 'fix' me (offering doctors from Cuba to Switzerland) and some did not mention it at all. Fewer still were clear-headed and practical. Various aunts and old chums seemed keen to underplay my state. 'You seem to be doing so well!' one offered. 'I mean, you can see something, can't you?' As I was to endlessly learn, few people understand the spectrum of sight loss.

I politely say that I have some functional sight, but there is only 15 per cent left of it, and it is declining. I spend many days trying to explain I am neither fully blind nor not blind – a strange limbo and twilight zone. Like Dante's Virgil, who walked through purgatory in his epic poem, being both means you know one world and the next – but don't belong to either. I was constantly asked

---

[2]Blindness and vision impairment (who.int) and Homepage. National Federation of the Blind (nfb.org).

questions: Do you want to be fixed and cured? And if not, why not? I didn't have a clear answer, but I did realize that I had to live with my 'blurry' reality, whether I liked it or not.

If I am feeling forthcoming or being playful, I can talk about the spectrum of blindness, or the various shades of grey blind people must deal with. Part of me always wants to give the full grown-up lecture that explains how there is a wide spectrum of sight and blindness, and most blind people live in varying degrees of shadows, light, dark, colour, foggy and fractured images. On the spectrum of severely sight impaired, but not completely blind, 217 million people in the world have moderate-to-severe vision impairment, of which I am one. But as I find myself increasingly exhausted at explaining these things, I usually offer to show people the extent of my vision. 'Cover your right eye completely with your right hand,' I say. 'Then take your left hand and turn it into a fist. Put the fist up in the centre of your left-hand vision, so it blocks your central sight. Now imagine the remaining sight murky and blurry, as if covered with Vaseline or clingfilm.' People do this, then nod in sympathy, and agree with me that I cannot see much.

If I am out and about with my white cane, I am often invited to discuss the difficulties of describing sight and blindness, sometimes about my own sight, but also about grannies, cousins, sisters and brothers, and friends. Many are confused that I prefer to describe the mystery of my sight loss in such a practical way. I explain that while my eye doctors can give me a very scientific description of how little sight I have – which is around 10–15 per cent, depending on the light – I don't find percentages particularly helpful. I do know that I can't see the tread of stairs or the edges of pavements, and can only read 26-size fonts on an adapted computer. I used text-to-speech software to write this book, which people find hard to imagine.

I also notice that often I am laden with other people's fantasies of what blindness and not seeing really means. We believe, for example, making love in the dark (yes, there is a word: *amavrophelia,* from the Greek, meaning love of darkness) will mean we have enhanced senses, especially touch. We even fetishize blindness – try looking up the word *occuphelia* (do NOT google on an office or home desktop, just in case the kids read it). Don't go there if you are squeamish. It made me wonder.

We are also constantly told blindness is a state to be fixed, because to live with it is so horrifying. Sighted writers have often indulged in this drama, and have used blindness to investigate love, relationships and power; notable authors such as Charles Dickens, Hans Christian Andersen, Charlotte Brontë, André Gide and, more recently, H. G.

Wells, John Wyndham and José Saramago have all devoted entire novels to blind characters who are saved by sighted heroes. Some are more deliberate than others. But even in fiction, blindness is endlessly presented as a tragic or heroic trope. Heaven forbid a blind character does something banal like the washing up.

So, as a woman losing her sight and dealing with the very mundane realities of day-to-day living, I began to wonder why there are so many myths about the words 'blind' and 'blindness' and the non-seeing condition. Why does blindness, or even any loss of sight, evoke so much feeling and emotion in us? My blindness called me to investigate further.

* * *

I am not the first to look at blindness in a historical context. Doctors, art historians, philosophers, writers, artists, sociologists, lawyers and many others have been engrossed in thinking about blindness ever since the ancient Egyptian sculptor from 4000 BC hammered hieroglyphics of blind harpists on the wall of his master's tomb to entertain him for eternity. Homer, the father of all Western narratives, was also said to be blind. Whether true or not, it's interesting that blindness was ascribed to him, even though there is no actual evidence. Many medical and academic scholars have also written clinical and eloquent works on the curing of blindness; there has been the representation of blindness in art; and philosophers and writers have debated empirical questions in philosophy and poetry. On a good day, blindness is intriguing and fascinating.

There is also an almost voyeuristic obsession with the blind person's personal memoir, even today. Owing to the assumption that blind lives are just so different, many blind authors have been lured (for funds and fame and sometimes, just feelings) to share their inner worlds in autobiographies – the most famous being writer and activist Helen Keller's *The Story of My Life* (1903), Aldous Huxley's *The Art of Seeing* (1942) and Ved Mehta's *Sound Shadows* (1986). More recently, there has been a spate of memoirs about incredible feats that blind people have engaged with. Among these have been Rachael Scdoris, the US dog musher and cross-country runner, who became the first blind person to complete the 1,600-kilometre Iditarod sled trail across Alaska, and Erik Weihenmayer, the US athlete and adventurer who is still the only blind person to have climbed Everest.

Even from a cursory scan, I found these memoirs have been hailed as symbols of triumph over adversity. A book in the 1950s about Louis Braille was reassuringly called *Triumph Over Darkness*, showing how blind people could 'overcome' their sightlessness just by having access to Braille. Even the one general history of blindness I found, written in 1952 by Dr Gabriel Farrell from Harvard University, consistently portrayed blindness and blind people in terms of polar extremes – inspirational or tragic – and in a tone that often seemed quite amazed that blind people could do anything at all. Sighted views of blindness are not very open-minded, it seemed.

Yet rarely throughout Western history have blind people been considered simply as, well, people who happen not to have sight. Rarely is blindness represented in a neutral, non-extreme way, rather than in terms of 'other'. This narrative has been perpetuated by mainly sighted historians; so much of our knowledge of blind people has relied on how sighted people have interpreted blindness. Somehow, as a society, we grant blindness far more drama than perhaps the physical state merits. We fear it, we punish with it and we find it powerful and alluring all at the same moment and have done so for centuries. More worryingly, we rarely hear the voices of blind people themselves. Why not? Who were these blind people who lived and died, who were not just heroes or burdens of the sighted world?

So, I wrote this book to investigate these questions, and hopefully offer a few answers.

* * *

Each chapter has two parts.

The first part is about my own journey into blindness. The other part is about actual historical events and blind people, and the way sighted people have interpreted blindness in different eras.

For me, this book is a conversation between past and present, part history and part memoir. Losing my sight prompted the beginning of my research, but my own experiences of blindness led me to investigate the 'how' and the 'why' of what blindness means, and has meant, and to explore new historical insights and voices. The journey has led me down many pathways, and I sense it will consume me for many years to come.

I chose to use my own, often difficult, blind experiences, woven in with historical knowledge, because I want to show how blindness and our reactions to it is still an active force in history. Each chapter relates an episode from my own life and shows how modern-day experiences are not so far-removed from the past – and that blindness is part of life, rather than separate, and always has been. I want to show that blindness infiltrates and impacts so much of our lives, but we have generally left this knowledge in the corridors of history. It is now time to let some new voices be heard and let loose into the mainstream.

Of course, in some ways I am writing this book for myself, to manage my own hopes and survival mechanisms. I want to know where we get our notions of blindness, why we still project them onto anyone with sight problems, and perhaps, with time, learn to accept them or push against them with grace and intelligence. I hope it will help all of us understand why we construct blindness as we currently do. Why is blindness so frightening? Or so inspiring? What makes us separate ourselves from our blind companions? And why aren't blind people part of our mainstream history, rather than a specialized and often academic subject? There certainly have been enough blind people around across the centuries to fill a few volumes.

Moreover, I want to chart how humanity's notion of blindness has changed over time. Somehow, the concept of blindness as a physical condition has been used continually as a marker and metaphor to reflect the era's own understandings of the human mind. In the Western hemisphere, at least, it has shaped many of our notions of society, truth, dark, good, evil, sex, religion, language, law, medicine and science. Whether bad or good, blindness has been endlessly portrayed and reported as something different, other and exceptional.

PROLOGUE

Blindness is interpreted in one of two ways: it either gives someone a superhuman status, with this 'specialness' perpetuated and ratified by sighted folk; or it is such a catastrophic tragedy that blind people are considered emblems of loss and pity. Such folk are considered burdens, defective, living in darkness. Under these terms, blind people are never simply people without sight; they can be geniuses and prophets, or considered blighted beings who live the most tragic lives, close to death. Even our notions of love are entwined with fantasies of blindness: we fall blindly in love and we make love in the dark, presumed to be more satisfying because our senses of touch, taste, hearing and smell are supposedly more heightened.

It goes without saying that I cannot speak for all blind people. As I am learning myself, there is a whole spectrum of sight loss, blindness, being blind, going blind and visual impairment, and I cannot capture all these experiences. What I can show is that blindness affects people in different ways and comes in many shapes, sizes and levels of blur. Some find sight loss an immense psychological and emotional trauma – whether being blind since birth or later in life. Many have understood how the dramatic ability of blinding someone is used by sighted powers to punish, considered second only to death. Losing your sight is complicated; it has both its advantages and its disadvantages, its good and bad days and, as I have discovered, some days that are just ordinary days, with a few adaptions.

So, the push behind this quest is to show how blindness matters and is an intrinsic part of influencing how we define ourselves, sighted or not. Blindness is omnipresent in our daily lives, now as in the past, and we don't acknowledge it enough – unless inspirational or tragic. As I sat in the libraries and blind educational establishments, I began to learn that our understanding of blindness has deeply influenced the present, and we need to hear more voices of blind people from the past to orientate and define ourselves in the present day. So this book will explore the lives of blind people, who have always been there but were simply left on the hillside of history because they did not fit the sighted world's purposes. Somehow, knowing others have been there before me has been very reassuring – blindness has been with us since time began.

In terms of stories and content, rather than trying to cover all blind stories, the book includes what I considered crucial turning points and blind people in Western history that best show the points I want to make. I know there are many more, and I will explore at another time the fascinating stories and ideas from China, India, Africa, Persia, Islamic states and beyond. For those who want more, there is a short bibliography at the end of the book as a starting place for reading. There are some seriously brilliant scholars out there who are giving disability history a more forceful voice than ever before and I encourage anyone to delve – it's amazing how much we do know, versus how much we don't.

A few words on language and vocabulary. For the purposes of this book, I will define and refer to blind people as people who have little functional sight, whether since birth or because of some event (usually disease, accident, war or punishment) in their lives. More importantly, I hope to show how we as a race are very 'ocularcentric' – a word to describe how we as humans describe the world in very sighted words. We use 'see' to say we understand. We use 'look' to emphasize an argument. We fall 'blindly' in love. We turn 'a blind eye' to mistakes and politicians' errors. One might even say we are 'blind' to ourselves in this matter.

I will also investigate the actual use of the words 'blind' and 'blindness' in terms of their European heritage and cultural origins. It was surprising to learn, for example, that the old Norse word 'blindr' and the Middle English 'blynde' are defined as 'deprived of sight' or 'to obscure sight' –

meanings we still understand today. Yet it is ironic that the word 'blynde' also meant a flash of light that could 'blynden someone', such as the light that struck Saul on the road to Damascus. The old Cockney phrase 'cor blimey', for example, is derived from a late twelfth-century saying, 'God blind me'. This literally meant 'Hide my eyes with God's great light, so I don't see evil.' Light and darkness can intermingle on so many levels, and ultimately, they are not opposites. As we will soon discover, so much of the experience of blindness is not binary – black and white – nor total all-encompassing darkness. Most of the time, it's a strange ambiguity of murkiness or blankness – it just is not seeing.

I can write this because I stand between seeing and not seeing, blur and clarity, colour and fud, and often feel my way with my cane and my hands and feet. Like many blind people, I still see something, even if just wedges of dim colour and movement around me. I don't have much functional eyesight. I can still read extra-large print if I tilt my head enough. I can get around with a cane, and a lovely husband whom I describe, much to his chagrin, as my 'guide dog'. I have special software and accessible tech to help me use my computer. And just for the record, I don't walk around with my arms stretched out, like a zombie in *Scooby-Doo*. Of those 36 million completely blind people in the world, we don't live in darkness, but simply don't see.[3]

But I also have to accept I am losing the ability to read my visual world. I am losing it, and there are certainly many days I miss looking, observing, gazing, resting my eyes on beauty and seeing. I particularly miss the colour blue – which I now see as a sort of dirty elephant grey – because blue calmed me and made my mind wander to oceans and lying on my back in wide open Mediterranean seas. I am now shifting to touch to gain that feeling of watching light on water, and it comes very often from simply holding someone's hand – which my beloved husband often does.

As I am writing this, 'Hello Darkness, My Old Friend', the song written by Simon and Garfunkel, has come on the radio in the background. The presenter is gushing over how Paul Simon wrote the song for his 'poor blind friend'. I checked the story on various websites,[4] and Art Garfunkel says that it is true that he wrote the song for his blind

---

[3] WHO Blindness and vision impairment (who.int).
Most blindness in the world today, including severe distance vision impairment, is due to unaddressed refractive errors (123.7 million), cataracts (65.2 million), glaucoma (6.9 million), corneal opacities (4.2 million), diabetic retinopathy (3 million), trachoma (2 million) or presbyopia (loss of ability to focus) (826 million).
[4] 'Hello Darkness, My Old Friend' recounts a blind man's friendship with Art Garfunkel – Jewish Telegraphic Agency (jta.org).

classmate Sandy Greenberg at college. He imagined, like perhaps you and I both did at the start of this book, that being blind is living in darkness.

The good news is blindness is not dark by a long way. And it never has been.

1

Imagining it

Nandy and mythic heroes

There once was a blind Neanderthal called Nandy, and he led me on a quest that I am not sure will ever be finished.

At an alumni dinner at my old university, some of my tutors asked how my eyesight was, as they knew I was losing my vision. In my usual perky voice, I said I was still a City reporter at the *Daily Telegraph* and that my eyesight was indeed getting worse. Sighs of empathy ran around the table. Always one to entertain, I regaled them with tales of my false eye – how when asking for an overdraft with a rather taciturn bank manager, my beautiful hand-painted Perspex false eye popped out and bounced across the shiny marble floor of the bank. The manager, speaking without a hint of irony, said very sternly, 'You will have to keep a better eye on your finances, Miss Mills', while I popped the eye back in, without a word, and he granted me the overdraft. The table erupted with laughter, and I sensed my impending blindness was eased, for myself and for them, by comedy.

We chewed our college chops and chatted convivially about other academic matters, but as we moved on to dessert, amongst the nods and mumblings of others who had overheard my eye story came friendly remarks such as 'Well done for keeping going' and even 'I am not sure how I would cope'. A few moments later, from further down the table a gruff-voiced male historian told me I was lucky to be losing my sight in the twenty-first century. 'In the nineteenth century', he said, with certitude, 'you would have been consigned to an institution or workhouse, or, if more fortunate, left at home in spinsterish solitude.' An eager, fresh young postgraduate medical student chimed in. 'Yes', she said cheerily, 'the blind certainly would not have met the fitness criteria of Darwinian theorists and you would more than likely have died from the workhouse or an infection after yet another quack intervention.' Everybody squirmed uncomfortably at the thought, me included, particularly at the phrase 'the blind' – as if we were all one homogeneous group, defined only by one disability.

'Oh, I don't know', said a friendly voice at the end of the table, belonging to a warm, round, stately archaeologist I had known for years. 'If you had been a Neanderthal, you might have been revered and treated with great honour – even outlived your sighted peers.' We sat and waited for more. She took a deep breath.

In 1961, in a cave in the Zagros Mountains, she told us, on the borders of Turkey and Iraq, a group of archaeologists[1] discovered the burial site of male skeletons dating to 50,000 years ago. One skeleton, officially called *Shanidar 1*, whom they nicknamed 'Nandy', showed signs of a crushing blow to the head and severe deformity, particularly in his ears and eye sockets. Modern methods of testing showed a bone disease which meant he would more than likely have been blind – surely a state that would have rendered him essentially immobile in a world of hunter-gathering.[2] Yet remarkably, unlike his peers who died in their late twenties, the carbon dating of Nandy proved that he had died when he was forty-five. 'Someone, somehow,' the professor said, enjoying our incredulity, 'had fed and watered blind Nandy.' We all nodded in respectful admiration, and the company at table diverged into chatting about other 'unknown'

---

[1] Crubézy, Eric, and Trinkaus, Erik. 'Shanidar 1: A case of hyperostotic disease (DISH) in the middle paleolithic'. *American Journal of Physical Anthropology* 89 (4) (December 1992): 411–420. doi:10.1002/ajpa.1330890402. PMID 1463085.
[2] https://www.smithsonianmag.com/arts-culture/the-skeletons-of-shanidar-cave-7028477/

archaeological discoveries in Wales and Africa. Then we moved onto cheese and port and other college matters.

As I returned to Cambridge's grey train station, tapping my cane across the platform and finding my seat with the help of a guard, I began to think about Nandy's existence. It was like receiving a faint wave from a distant relative. Nandy's story was part of man's identity as much as hunting, gathering, eating, sleeping and loving. Just knowing Nandy, as a blind being, had lived and most likely functioned with blindness 50,000 years ago gave me a sense of a shared human experience – a connection that was wholly cheering. Despite my postprandial haze, I found myself thinking how even the smallest facet of new information can shift your perception of the past in an instant.

One thing puzzled me, though. The warm, round archaeologist had told us there was no evidence to show how other Neanderthals had engaged with Nandy. We don't know if he received a special burial, or simply died where he had lived, in the outer edges of the cave. There were no odes, images or graffiti on the cave walls. So how did the esteemed professor know, or even imagine, that Nandy was revered, as she mentioned? Why did we, a bunch of over-educated, well-intentioned folks, presume to go along with this idea? After all, maybe Nandy had simply been a greedy, grungy, boring grunter who happened to live by a berry tree or a river which sustained him in his later life. If he was fed and cared for, maybe it was simply because everyone shared their bounty? Was Nandy so special simply because he was blind? Why have historians treated the topic of blindness with so such fascination, fear and reverence? Sadly, there is not much information about Nandy, and we have no record of his voice nor graffiti from the past. But such questions still lingered.

* * *

As usual, intellectual ponderings were overtaken by the demands of daily life, and I reverted to my job as a financial news journalist. I moved on to think of other things like stocks and shares, and self-important CEOs. On days off, I did consider whether I might write a nice 'personal think piece' on the presumptions of blindness or interview a famous blind person or two (Stevie Wonder and Andrea Bocelli came to mind). I was even commissioned to write a big feature in the *Guardian*[3] about the then home secretary, David Blunkett, who had an affair with an editor at the *Spectator*. The press was full of the assumption that his blindness was part of his allure because he must surely have a heightened sense of touch and smell, and this was how he attracted women. But maybe he was just a nice

---

[3] 'What's Blindness Got To Do With It?' *Guardian*, 8 December 2004.

bloke, I argued, who was charming, clever and good in bed. It might have been nothing to do with being blind and everything to do with a certain skill set.

But what if one was *not* a hot blind lover? What if, as I lost my sight, I was not compensated with gifts of better hearing, taste, smell and touch? What if I was just, well, like everyone else? My thoughts went back to Nandy – what if he simply was someone who could not see, rather than someone set apart for others to revere? After a few months, and in a bid to discover more, I signed up for a desk at the British Library and, with the help of the erudite team, created lists of blind people, whether fictional or real, who lay beneath the surface of mainstream history, or had featured in the hero-worshipping attitudes of Western culture.

As to be expected, the list included a fair number of white men, a few women, and a large whiff of blindness either having mythical properties or burdensome tragedy. First came the itinerant monks, priests and occasional nuns who experienced miracle moments because of their blindness. Then came blind emperors, blind princes and kings, and the odd blind scholar who could afford secretaries. Blind senators and soldiers featured too, riding into battle, guided and held in place by their men and horses. By the nineteenth century, there were lists of extraordinary blind achievers and campaigners, not to mention a slew of religious writers, professors and composers. Then came a plethora of blind musicians, as well as literary and academic giants, who gained fame via the newly flourishing world of the press and the love of jazz.

The narrative arc each time was very clear: if blindness was mentioned, it was because it had been 'overcome', and thus blind heroes were superhuman. As usual, men seemed to outrank women in these lists, but it was also clear that blind people have been part of the general lot of humanity over millennia owing to congenital disease, age, war, accident or punishment. It struck me, too, that there seem to be a disproportionate number of historical 'achievers' of all kinds who are blind, in comparison with the general population.

Indeed, until the invention of Braille (raised print) in the mid-nineteenth century, most blind people had no access to reading and writing at all, unless wealthy enough to hire staff or an amanuensis, or to be in a religious environment where notes could be dictated. But whether by a blind author or not, I repeatedly found blindness depicted and reported as something different, other, and usually economically connected to how disadvantaged blind people were. This 'otherness' was not only perpetuated in myths and legend but also, more recently, in biography, fiction and film, even by blind people themselves – a sort of internalization of what sighted people wanted blind people to be.

*   *   *

As I sat in my little booth in the British Library, what emerged was that previous histories of blindness had been written by sighted people for sighted people, with little attention to the voices of blind people themselves. In order to investigate, I would have to take a new view on blind history; I would have to search as far back as possible and in different arenas. Importantly, I would have to grapple with how stories about blindness did not fit together in a seamless linear fashion.

In fact, what I fundamentally needed to grasp was that the history of blindness was not one single story, and no one blind or sighted person could own it. Interpretations of blindness need to be plaited together to reflect the broader themes and belief systems of each age, rather that fitted into a neat package. I also had to consider how to find authentic blind voices and lives from the past, told on their own terms. How did blind people perceive how they were treated, and how did they own or control their own lives? Perhaps such voices would be impossible to find, but I had to try. As many historians have said, we may have the same human passions and flaws as our predecessors, but our preconceptions, preoccupations and priorities have so often been very different.[4]

Finally, where did I fit into this complex mosaic of ideas and imaginings? Where, as a woman losing her sight, did I place myself in this twenty-first-century visual world, and could I have thrived, or even survived, in the past?

* * *

While there is no one exact link or explanation as to why blindness is so often perceived as such an exceptional state, in the Western hemisphere at least, it has always had mythical and exceptional qualities attributed to it. Whether it be inspiration prophecy or even a state of catastrophe, there is something about not seeing, in a world of seeing, that has made blindness separate, brilliant and extremely powerful. The first person we know placed in this tradition of blind geniuses, and who holds this exceptional blind power, is the so-called father of Western literature and poet supreme, Homer.

As the playwright Aeschylus wrote, all other literary works have been 'slices from the great banquets of Homer', and almost all biographies of Homer tell us that he was blind. The general consensus is that Homer, the man, lived

---

[4]Murray, Douglas. 'History is Less Clear as You are Living Through it.' *Spectator*, 1 January 2022, p. 51.

between the eighth and seventh centuries BC, but the epic compositions that we know so well were not just created by him, but composed by a collective group of poets (both men and women) who all had a major hand in *The Odyssey* and *The Iliad*. While details of Homer's actual life remain murky, what we do know is that the notion of Homer as blind was a consistent, well-marinated 'brand' handed down from generation to generation,[5] and that blind characters appear throughout his most famous works. In book VIII of *The Odyssey*, the faithful bard comes in, led by a page: 'The Muse had favoured him above all others, yet had given him good and evil mingled. His eyes she took from him, but she gave him entrancing song.'[6]

We also hear about Homer being blind from other famous writers and historians. Three hundred years after Homer's death, Thucydides tells us that he was 'a blind man, dwelling on the rocky island of Chios'. Herodotus and Aristotle also took up the baton, particularly connecting blindness to talent, referring to Homer as 'blind, but seeing'. Some classicists have remarked that his name meant 'blindness' in a particular local dialect. Archaeologists have

---

[5] Flower, Attyah Michael, *The Seer in Ancient Greece* (University of California Press, 2009).
[6] Homer, Oxford World Classics, *The Odyssey*, Book VIII (Oxford University Press), p. 86.

also dug up labelled statues of Homer from the fifth and sixth centuries AD, and his bust consistently portrays him with eyes half shut – an ancient suggestion of age or sight loss, perpetuating the idea of the blind poet-hero of the classical world. I wish I had known this when I was at the Pergamon Museum in Berlin a few years ago, which is bulging with Homeric statues.

But was Homer blind? And why should we care?

It is intriguing to see how we and quite a few poets and scholars have pondered this question, given the limited evidence and records, and the myths that have built up over the years. Some reject the premise Homer was blind at all, and suggest instead that he was a sighted bard known for telling his stories while floating in a reverie. This thesis was well articulated back in the 1930s, when two Harvard professors, Milman Parry and Albert Lord, saw (and filmed) how Balkan singers threw themselves into rhapsodic trances in telling great traditions and stories. These proved, they said, Homer's 'blindness', and stories of his eyes being half-closed were accounts of a man in a trance, not a man who could not see.

Other scholars and writers have disagreed and argued that Homer's brand of blindness being attached to his name was a way of gaining a unique reputation – a clever PR strategy for the audience to think of the poet in awe and to directly connect him to the gods on Mount Olympus. They argued that thousands of blind people across Europe and Asia made a living as minstrels, musicians and storytellers. Adding the label 'blind' to the label 'poet' connected the storyteller to an intimate knowledge of an all-powerful set of deities and a knowledge of a different kind. After all, if – as Herodotus, the grandfather of history, tells us – Zeus gave Euenius the amazing faculty of divination in exchange for his sight, why would a blind poet *not* take up the blind branding?

Renaissance blind poets have also attached themselves to the Homeric blind bandwagon. The seventeenth-century poet, polyglot and freedom fighter John Milton, for example, composed many of his epic works, such as *Paradise Lost*, while he had sight. But when he became blind and wrote poetry about his sight loss, it is interesting how his blindness, more than his actual talent, became his calling card. His most poignant poem, 'On his Blindness', became the mawkish banner of nineteenth-century sentimentality. Its opening lines are well known:

When I consider how my light is spent,
Ere half my days, in this dark world and wide,
And that one Talent which is death to hide
Lodged with me useless, though my Soul more bent[7]

---

[7] Milton, John. Sonnet 19, 'On His Blindness'. Poetry Foundation.

I have had quite a few debates with friends over Milton's view of blindness. I do find it a sentimental and mournful verse, equating blindness with darkness and loss. I don't think of blind people as 'those who stand and wait', as is written at the end of the sonnet. Others disagree, arguing it is an ode to serving one's God, and that Milton is saying it doesn't matter what or who you are, we all 'stand and wait'. But whatever one's interpretation of the poem, the myth of blind Milton has lasted, like Homer, well into the present era as a template for talent owing to the loss of sight.

The presumption that blindness grants its owner special status has been regularly used to explain many poets' success. Here are the words of the nineteenth-century wit and playwright Oscar Wilde:

I have sometimes thought that the story of Homer's blindness might be really an artistic myth created in critical days to remind us not merely that the great poet is always a seer, seeing less with the eyes of the body than he does with the eyes of the soul, but he is a true singer also, building his song out of music, repeating each line over and over again 'til he has caught the secret of its melody, chanting in the darkness the words that are winged with light.[8]

---

[8]Wilde, Oscar. *Essays on Aesthetics* (https://listentogenius.com/author.php/171).

Like others before him, Wilde seems to be suggesting that anything that enhances talent, such as being compensated by exceptional memory or hearing, only adds to an artist's reputation. Blindness emphasized how Homer was sensitive to language, rhythm and the musicality of words. Wilde argued that poets convert words into images in our heads, and blindness, or the idea of blindness, made that even more possible. I find it fascinating that these great minds perpetuate the myths of heightened senses and special talent coming as a direct result of blindness.

Twentieth-century blind poets have continued the tradition by attaching themselves to the blind myth. The father of modernist poetry, T. S. Eliot (1888–1965), places the character of Tiresias centre stage of his poem *The Waste Land* because, despite being non-seeing, he could comment on the action and the ever-transitional nature of man. As a blind seer, he is a useful plot device: he is seeing and not seeing, male and female. He says this in the opening lines: 'I Tiresias, though blind, throbbing between two lives'. Eliot explains, in his notes on his work,[9] that the not-seeing aspect allows a hero to

---

[9]'Tiresias, although a mere spectator and not indeed a "character", is yet the most important personage in the poem, uniting all the rest. Just as the one-eyed merchant, seller of currants, melts into the Phoenician Sailor, and the latter is not wholly distinct from Ferdinand Prince of Naples, so all the women are one woman, and the two sexes meet in Tiresias. What Tiresias sees, in fact, is the substance of the poem.' *The Waste Land* by T. S. Eliot with Annotations (windingway.org).

belong to past and present, not to mention providing a unique and memorable selling point.

The Nobel prize-winning Argentinian poet Jorge Luis Borges (1899–1986) also argued that blindness figured as a special state that grants its owner talent and skill. Borges, who became blind later in his life, wrote in his essay 'Blindness' that there was a great irony in being a man of letters, indeed becoming the director of the National Library of Argentina, without sight. Like Oscar Wilde and T. S. Eliot, he argued that as a blind poet, there was something mysterious and visionary about blindness. There was 'something harmonious' between writing and blindness, he wrote, and the fact there were quite a few great blind writers was not a coincidence. Blindness, he was implying, allowed him access to a world beyond the real world we all occupy.

Recently, however, blind writers have rebelled against such mythical thinking. Professor Georgina Kleege, herself blind, rejects the connection on the basis that as a blind person it sets up unrealistic expectations and perpetuates the myth of superhuman blind people.[10] Why can't blind people be, well, just non-seeing?

I am inclined to agree.

* * *

---

[10]Kleege, Georgina. *Sight Unseen* (Yale University Press, 1999).

If Homer's blindness cult was not enough for me to indulge in 'hero' worshipping of blind poets and spiritual guides, other ancient myths and blind fictional characters certainly added to the pot of blind glory. The most famous blind character with whom we still associate visions, prophetic knowledge and wisdom is the fictional seer and prophet Tiresias. Like Homer, Tiresias' sight loss is directly connected to the divine and his misuse of sight. In one explanation of how Tiresias becomes blind, we are told it is because he is caught spying on the goddess Athena in her bath. In Callimachus' poem 'The Bathing of Pallas', Tiresias is blinded by Athena after he 'stumbled' upon her bathing. His mother, Chariclo, who was a nymph of Athena, begged Athena to undo her curse. Sadly, she could not, but instead she cleaned his ears and gave him the ability to understand birdsong and thus the gift of augury – foretelling the future – which brings him fame and notoriety. In another telling – my favourite, told by Hesiod – Tiresias finds himself in the middle of a domestic tiff between the gods Zeus and Hera, where they are arguing over who has more pleasure during sex. Tiresias claims women have the better time. Outraged that Tiresias has revealed a woman's deepest secret, Hera takes his eyesight. Zeus, delighting in his wife's discomfort but unable to undo her curse, gives Tiresias the gift of prophecy. The moral of both tales is that earthly sight can lead you into trouble, an idea that continued well into the Middle Ages. In the late 1280s, in the time of Edward II of England, raping or assaulting a woman was punished by tearing out the eyes and chopping off the testicles to mitigate, according to the statutes of the time, 'the appetite which entered through the eyes, and the heat of fornication'.

It also cheered me, as a woman with one eye, to find a few Western gods who had one eye (who were not so pleasant – more later) in the ancient Greek myths, but also notably in Viking ones in northern Europe. The Norse god-in-chief – usually called Odin or Wodin – was also called 'Blindr'. This was because, the story goes, Odin loses part of his physical sight deliberately to gain access to sacred wisdom. He gouges out his own eye to be given permission to drink from the Well of Wisdom at the root of the World Tree, Yggdrasil. The profligate god then drops his eye into the well, where it remains as a token of his sacrifice. As a result, he sees more with his one eye than he ever did with two. As with Tiresias, this Nordic story makes a direct connection between blindness and wisdom via a direct transaction: a physical eye for a spiritual one. Nobody says outright 'sacrificing your eye is on a level with all knowledge', but the implication is that they are both things that only a true candidate for Top God status can win. By achieving blindness, Blindr gains understanding beyond the normal mortal scope. Indeed, he threw down his one eye for his people.

For a while, I loved reading these stories and commentaries, and floated away on a magical carpet of blind genius. I loved the idea that in these epic ancient works, blindness was portrayed as a gift and blessing, rather than a burden or suffering, and for five minutes I thought I could be part of this canon – lack of genius notwithstanding. After Nandy, it seemed a group of blind men (and possibly women) were responsible for some of the most important artistic material in the world.

I also wondered, as I read these ancient and exceptional stories (and remembering they were fictional), whether the attachment of blindness to talent made complete sense from a sighted perspective. Why not have a blind character who can see into the future, and help speed up the plot? Why not have a blind man as the voice that can describe what the audience cannot see, just as we cannot see? Metaphorically, at least, aren't we always 'blind' to what happens in the next stage or the next page, as we are all blind to the future?

But here's my problem: what if you don't have talent? What if you can't write beautiful odes? Are you stuck forever as the most boring blind person in the world? And how does the world interpret your blindness? Are you doomed? By removing the ability to 'gaze' upon someone, why are you removing the ability to be acknowledged and recognized?

* * *

As well as the stories of Homer the 'blind genius poet' and Tiresias the prophet seer, other writers also used blindness to denote the most terrifying and feared earthly punishments. Blindness was the perfect fate for those who betrayed the gods or their family – a fate worse than death. In this rendition of blindness, the blind person could never see their children or loved ones again, in this world or the next.

One of the most vivid and shocking of these fictions is the self-imposed blinding by King Oedipus in Sophocles' play *Oedipus Rex*, written around 400 BC. Here Oedipus, having slept with his mother and killed his father, discovers himself to be the cause of a plague in Thebes, even though the mystical blind seer Tiresias (whom we met in the exceptional blind category) vehemently warns him not to investigate. Oedipus' choice of castigation is not to kill himself or to cut off the offending organ (possibly a more suitable option, given his crimes), but to take his own sight. We hear about his self-blinding from his servant, allowing us to imagine the worst, rather than see it.

SERVANT:
And then he shouted at his eyes
These eyes will never see the light again, never
Cursing his two blind eyes over and over, he

Lifted the brooches again and drove their pins through his eyeballs up
To the lids until they were pulp, until the blood streamed out
Soaking his beard and cheeks,
A black storm splashing its hail across his face

It is a shocking scene which has struck readers and poets for centuries – 'a black storm' (his own blood) splashing across his face. Here stands a man, fully aware of the consequences of his actions, completely exposed in front of his people in the fullness of his agony and shame. Later, Oedipus, blind and alone on stage, explains this eye removal is a 'just' punishment because he will not have the joy of seeing his real parents or even his children again. Blindness thus becomes comparable and close to death, the ultimate closure on life – an image that easily affects the audience, and an enduring legacy for reading blindness for centuries to come.

Even one-eyed monsters got in on the gore, particularly in the grizzly case of the Cyclopes. The story of young Odysseus landing on the island of the one-eyed Cyclopes as he returns home from the Trojan Wars is brutal. Entering the cave home of the one-eyed giant Polyphemus, Odysseus and his men become trapped. Polyphemus then eats two of

Odysseus' soldiers as a light snack. In a postprandial daze, he asks his guests their names, and Odysseus says he is called 'Nobody'. Unconcerned, our one-eyed monster heads out to tend his sheep, leaving Odysseus and his men in the cave. Upon his return, our hero offers the giant a large cup of intoxicating wine, which sends him off into a deep sleep. In a leap of bravery, Odysseus plunges a large wooden stake into the giant's eye. On awakening, Polyphemus shouts for help from his fellow giants, saying that 'Nobody' has hurt him. Of course, the other Cyclopes, hearing what they think are the rantings of a mad beast, conclude that Polyphemus has been afflicted by divine power and recommend prayer as the answer.

Odysseus and his men escape the next morning, tying themselves to the underbellies of the local sheep and avoiding the exploring touch of the Cyclops as the sheep leave the cave. As he sails off with his men, Odysseus boastfully reveals his real name, an act of hubris that will cause problems for him later. Yet again, we are being told, whether one-eyed or two, the key to revenge is to remove the ability to see.

Other classical playwrights, including Euripides, Aristophanes and Virgil, took up the same plot device of blindness to elicit fear and pathos in their audience. Perhaps the most tragic is Euripides (424 BC) narrating the actions of Hecuba, Queen of Troy. As usual in Greek tragedy, revenge is the pivot of the story. In a time after the Trojan Wars, Hecuba sends her son Polydorus, with vast quantities of jewellery and gold, away from their war-torn city to stay with an ally, King Polymestor. The king betrays her by drowning the young man and keeps the loot for himself. Stricken with grief and anger, despite the fact she has eighteen other children, Hecuba lures Polymestor back to Troy with promises of more gold. When he arrives, she presents him with his children, who are then killed one by one in front of him by the women of Troy. Hecuba herself then claws out his eyes, leaving him humiliated and swaying on the stage on all fours, 'a mountain beast'. As Hecuba explains, she chose his eyes because through his actions he no longer has the right to see the love of another's gaze. Worse still, he is left with the image of his murdered children as the last thing he sees. Hecuba's revenge is complete. Euripides explains the act simply: 'She blinds him because blind he always was.'[11] Despite such gore, she manages to continue her adventures and is later turned into a dog, as she snarls and curses at Odysseus. Not exactly cheery reading.

---

[11] Euripides. *Hecuba*. Translated by E. P. Coleridge. Revised by Casey Dué and Mary Ebbott. Based on the Greek text as edited by James Diggle (Oxford, 1994).

* * *

As I read through this plethora of punishing gore, what was hard to absorb was that, away from genius and prophecy, it was clear how blindness has consistently separated and alienated people, whether heroes or demons. Even in the supposedly more enlightened nineteenth century, full of advances and great changes for blind people – education, employment, Braille and philanthropy – history and social commentary also perpetuated the burden and tragedy of blindness, the words 'blind' and 'beggar' frequently sitting side by side. If blindness was not a punishment in name, it certainly was in practice.

We are not free of this fear even today. As my young American nephews point out to me, extreme notions of blindness are still prevalent in modern-day superhero movies. Dive into any streaming service and you will find a plethora of blind heroes. Marvel's Dare Devil is a blind barrister by day, but by night a superhero vigilante with special senses for fighting crime. In the third film of the *Matrix* franchise, Neo is blinded so he can understand the Matrix. The BBC splashed on its front news page the arrival of a blind man at the top of Everest – impressive, if a bit chilly.

Even if a blind person is not portrayed as a superhuman, their functioning in the world, even normally, is worthy of a

TV series; for example, *In the Dark*, in which a blind young woman tries to solve her friend's murder. As I write this paragraph, I can hear my husband listening to the Paralympics in Tokyo, the commentary of which contains a deluge of inspiration and chirpiness around the reportage of blind swimmers, runners and javelin throwers. These days blindness is so much more than not seeing; so often it is about stretching the boundaries of human endurance.

Watch, too, the crop of charity adverts on commercial TV channels and note how you are told how awful it is to have a blind life. Some non-profits even ask sighted people to blindfold themselves and have a friend give them an unidentified amount of cash and then attempt to pay for a meal with this money, allegedly proving just how hard and onerous the blind life is. One charity asks people to take care of their child for one minute while blindfolded, suggesting it is such a dangerous and difficult task for a blind person that no one should risk it. Indeed, my life as a blind person is presumed to be so lonely that someone on Twitter recently messaged me to say that I should have a free Bible Audio player,[12] specially designed for me because I was losing sight. (Are sighted people not afforded such generosity?) I could go on with the list, but these are illustration enough.

---

[12] www.torchtrust.org

In many ways, the way blindness has been represented, even by the greats, makes me feel lonely and depressed; comparing the depictions of blind people in antiquity and today seems to foster a sense that little has changed. To add to this, I had so little in common with these fantastical myths. I did not feel particularly close to any of the depictions. Even from a cursory look at classical times, I began to realize how little we understand blindness and sight loss, and that we make so many assumptions about what it means to be blind. If I was not superhuman, these mythic stories told me, I was worthless.

* * *

Occasionally, serendipity leads you to surprising new thinking, and in the same way that an alumni dinner at Cambridge led me to Nandy, and Nandy led me to the library, so too the hours in the library led me to get backache, and a need to take a break from the books. After a coffee, I crossed over to the British Museum to have a feel of the Parthenon Marbles – who knew there used to be an entire model of them, in relief, for blind people to feel and enjoy? I had a happy hour stroking the raised casts of the horses' and soldiers' features.

While I was fondling a horse's head, a guide approached me and asked if I had touched the votives in another room.

We strolled over to an adjacent chamber, and she left me there. Should you ever have ten minutes free in the British Museum, go and see the Roman eye-votives. Created by and for their owners to ask the gods to heal eye infections, disease and accidents, there are hundreds of beautifully carved stone eyes, calling upon the gods to help their mothers, fathers, children or slaves to regain sight. Even if votives are not your thing, they are a wonderful reminder that blindness was not all glory or gore, but often something in the mainstream, and part of human daily life. Many more arguments like this have been taken up by scholars of late, possibly to counter the fictitious gory/glory image of blindness.

Indeed, far more blind people have been part of ordinary classical life than the rarefied plots and myths that informed the plays and poems of Homer, Sophocles and Euripides. Blind people would have been very much part of the audience that watched and listened to the epics. As Professor Martha Rose has argued in her seminal volume *The Staff of Oedipus*,[13] blind people – more than the sighted audience – would understand the references to the horror of blindness, but also understood it as a condition that could happen to anyone, at any time.

---

[13]Rose, Martha. *The Staff of Oedipus: Transforming Disability in Ancient Greece* (University of Michigan Press, 2003).

Professor Rose also pointed out that eyes, and fixing of the eyes, were frequently discussed in medical tracts that referred to blindness as a condition that might be treated. Galen, the personal physician to several Roman emperors around the fourth century AD, wrote volumes describing the eye, its function and use; he created terms such as cornea, retina and conjunctiva, which we still use today. Those, along with chronic disease, congenital malformation, accident, and the normal ageing process, made blindness something that almost certainly affected millions of people. The historian Herodotus writes that even the famed Egyptian pharaoh Sesostris went 'blind like his father', Pheron. The revered first-century AD biographer and historian Plutarch claimed of King Timoleon that it was a 'predisposition of his family to lose their sight preceding death'. Blindness was simply a part of everyday life.

Blindness even had intellectual currency as a subject worthy of debate and consideration. In Aristotle's *Parva Naturalia,* a collection of short treatises written in the fourth century BC which examined the nature of the body, the soul and related phenomena, he declared blind people were usually more 'intelligent' than deaf people, as thought processes (and thus intelligence) were generated from audible sounds. What was reassuring about this type of research, despite it often being dense and heavy to read (not to mention unhelpfully and inaccurately positing deafness against blindness), was that these were not the stories of triumph over adversity, special powers or terrible fates, but stories showing that blindness has always been with us. From early on we have found ways to accept and adapt to the realities of it. No more, no less.

* * *

So here I was, in the British Library at the beginning of the twenty-first century: a woman with a hand-painted false eye and diminishing sight in her other eye, who had never defined herself as blind – or even visually impaired – but was now confronted with irreversible sight loss and the expectation by her culture and historical legacy that her life would be either one of super heroic feats or disastrous tragedy. In between, there were myriad different narratives of blindness piling up on my library desk. I now had a head full of mythic Greek and Roman blind characters who set up unrealistic expectations for someone like me in the present day.

Did I feel closer to understanding my impending blindness and accepting how other sighted people treated me? Did I feel better that stories about prehistoric Nandy and the others were considered part of all our histories? To be honest, not really; I was still confused and realized I had taken on a mammoth task. I even found myself doubting whether I wanted to continue the project. My own Odyssey could involve depressing stories that might not help me come to terms with my own blindness, and possibly make me suffer at the enormity of human indifference and cruelty. On the other hand, there could be new stories to discover that could give me, and others, a new identity. Blindness was not just one state – it was many states.

So I pressed on, because it was clear there was not one linear version of history and none of the stories about blindness would fit together as a seamless whole. In fact, perhaps the first lesson I learnt from my gentle audit of classical times was that blindness, both as an idea and a physical state, is interpreted entirely through the context and era in which it is lived – and usually from a sighted point of view.[14]

In a sense, those first months in the library showed me that interpretations of blindness needed to be woven together to reflect the broader themes and belief systems of each age, rather than fitting into a neat package. What I learnt from those early days in the library was that blindness was an active force in society, and has shaped law, politics, medicine, science, sex, art, war and peace.

Part of my quest, which Nandy the Neanderthal had initiated and my own loss of sight in the twenty-first century had influenced, would be to compile, sieve and digest as much as possible, to find a different way to see blindness.

---

[14] Farrell, Gabriel. *The Story of Blindness* (Harvard University Press, 2014).

2

Living with it

Dark versus light

*And God said, 'Let there be light,' and there was light.
God saw that the light was good, and he separated
the light from the darkness.
God called the light 'day,' and the darkness he called 'night'.*

GENESIS 1.3–5 (KJV)

Long before hearing about Nandy the Neanderthal, misfiring my fork to find food on a plate from lack of sight, or even bumping into walls, tables and lampposts, I lived in the Holy City of Rome, where I worked as a journalist for Reuters news agency.

In this most beautiful and visual of cities, I began to understand that, possibly since Nandy first started grunting, or the mythic Oedipus wrenched his eyes out of his sockets, there has been the deep assumption that a blind life is, or will be, a journey of abject misery and suffering. Blindness is a state that is considered by many religions, including Christianity, to be a deficit and a burden, and very clearly a separate state to be deeply pitied.

To be honest, I spent most of my time in Rome feeling as if I was floating between a Henry James novel or a Fellini film – often at the same time. I loved walking to work in the early warm mornings, sniffing the miasma of melons, tomatoes and fresh basil from the markets. I spent many days watching nuns fly past on bicycles by my office window or listening to young American tourists yelling across the piazzas in the evenings. I did not even mind random nuns cooing over me as I sometimes stumbled, gestured to find a wall or fell. I would explain I had '*problemi di occhi*', pointing to my eyes. Their sighs and tilting of heads, and cries of '*poverina*' and '*carissima*', felt entirely normal in a city jam-packed with holy folk with a penchant for prayer.

Occasionally, I used my white cane and sported fake designer sunglasses from the market, which I thought might help me navigate a bit more safely. But whenever I did, quite a few nuns would stop me in the street or café and, without asking me, caress my face or stroke my hair. Some folks even offered me on-the-spot prayers (often to St Lucia or St Bridget, the patron saints of light and sight) and it left me wondering if I should stroke their hair or squeeze their cheeks back.

During my first month in Rome, I was told by a kind priest whom I met in the piazza overlooked by a statue of Giordano Bruno, a man burnt at the stake for believing the sun went around the earth, that a special mass had been held for my failing sight at the Venerable English College (where Roman Catholic English priests train). The whole college had prayed for me. I was deeply embarrassed, not only because I am not a believer of sorts, but I felt there were others far more in need of help.

By month two, a cute Scottish journalist asked me on a date, but on hearing my eyesight issues were not fixable, he almost burst into tears. Hardly containing himself, he sniffed: 'You are such a wee lamb ... why did this have to happen to you?' Wee I am not, and I was shocked at receiving pity for a physical problem I had absolutely no control over. The date was quickly cut short – by me.

After the weeping Scot, I became acquainted with my local friendly Swedish nun, with whom I would queue and gossip at the local bakery about such important things as what to do with sage in one's cooking (you melt the butter and then add it, so it doesn't burn). All was going well, until she one day asked about my eyesight. A few weeks later, she gushingly told me that her 'sisters' would continue to pray for my sight at the Swedish Convent at the Angelus (the waking bell every morning). It was all rather too much.

Who was this poor and pitiable person they were praying for? And why would I need such prayers? It was confusing. Where did this sense of deficit come from? Why did blindness ignite pity?

In other words, when did we decide that light was – and is – a metaphorical touchstone for truth, and darkness a symbol of death and decay? Perhaps unsurprisingly, birth, life and death come a great deal into it.

* * *

From our earliest sense of ourselves, lack of sight and light have been a very useful metaphor to understand where we come from and have been woven into so many creation myths.

The difference between light and dark, seeing and not seeing, or between one thing and another has been a useful way to explain how life, and our very existence, comes from the emergence of light. Many cultures, such as the ancient Egyptians, believed the sun came directly from the mound or from a lotus flower that grew from the mound, in the form of a heron, falcon, scarab beetle or human child. In other stories, Japanese myths said light particles came from a beaten and shapeless matter and rose, while sounds sank down. The Hindu festival of Diwali signifies the victory of light over darkness, good over evil, knowledge over ignorance, and hope over despair. In the traditional homeland of the Navajo, in North America, the mists of light arise through the darkness to animate and bring purpose in the lower worlds.

Closer to my own Judeo-Christian heritage, the Jewish festival of lights, Hanukkah, celebrates the victory of the Maccabees over the Syrian Greek army. The Rabbinic tradition states the Maccabees could only find enough oil to keep the commemorative Menorah lit for one night, but it stayed alight for eight days. Light conquers even an oil shortage.

A less spiritual description of darkness, given to me by scientist friends, defines it as the absence of light – a dark object absorbs photons, making it seem invisible to other objects with light and colour. In the art world, this absence is used to denote presence. If used in a positive way, for example in painting methods such as *chiaroscuro*, darkness is made to make us focus our attention on the action or person illuminated; it means that anything in the darkness is not seen much, if at all. Even the origin of the word 'dark' comes from the old Germanic *'tarnen'*, meaning to conceal. Perhaps because of the need to bury our dead underground, or the notion of hell being below us, darkness has never had a good press.

Light, on the other hand, has been the creator and genesis of everything. Light, according to the assumed binary opposition, allows man and womankind to find a mate, hunt, fish, plant and survive on the earth. It allows humans to share knowledge (first by hieroglyphics, later printed matter and now digital screens), avoid danger and even find love by spying a desirable mate. Light, and thus sight, is the sense that above all allows us to live. Closer to home, the Judeo-Christian creation myth is all about the light separating from the dark. For in the beginning, as the very first book in the Bible tells us, 'God said, "Let there be light," and there was light'. And the thing about the light was that it was good. It therefore determined that 'darkness' was bad, even before the sun separated from the moon on the fourth day of creation.

With this clear and binary division between light and dark, good and evil, knowledge and ignorance, it is hardly surprising that blindness, as portrayed in the Bible, became an emblem of foreboding, concealment and ignorance – and above all, of spiritual absence. In Leviticus, for example, the Lord informs Moses of those bodily imperfections, including blindness, lameness and a flat nose (who knew?), that shall prevent people from being part of sacred rituals or approaching the altar in the synagogue. The story of Sodom and Gomorrah even tells us how angels blinded people trying to have same-gender sex. To be blinded, in the Old Testament, was a severe misfortune or punishment, but was rarely neutral or useful.

* * *

This notion of light and dark, good versus evil, and truth versus lies permeated the more hopeful arrival of Christianity and ran through the guide to being a good Christian. In the New Testament, sight and blindness were pitted against each other, whether in physical or written form, particularly as Christianity became more widespread and formalized during medieval times.

Across Europe, people from rich to poor were familiar with allegorical statues and stained-glass images of blind and seeing women, known as *Ecclesia* and *Synagoga*, many of which decorate the porticos of the great French cathedrals. My favourites are in Chartres and Notre Dame in Paris. At first glance, both images of the poised women look the same. Each stand side by side, regally dressed and holding a lance. Such images appeared across Europe from the twelfth century onwards and are occasionally found in illuminations and texts. Yet if you look carefully, *Ecclesia*, representing the Church, stands a little bit straighter, carries an unbroken sword and stares wide-eyed at the onlooker. Conversely, *Synagoga* is blindfolded and thus ignorant, holds a damaged sword displaying her loss, and is often little bit hunched in humility. By the thirteenth century, not only did the blindfold appear on *Synagoga*, but on any figure who did not accept and thus 'see' the arrival of Christ. Stand in front of the main doors of these cathedrals, and just on the left, at the threshold, is the ultimate Christian notion of blindness that people saw every day.

For the minority of literate and educated souls, and particularly for those who read the New Testament, there are also frequent references to blindness as being a terrible state. In Matthew 15, people are told to leave blind people as there is no hope for them: 'Leave them; for they are blind and leaders of the blind; for if a blind mind offers to lead a blind man, they will fall into the pit together.' Blindness was, therefore, a useful metaphor for spiritual blindness, and thus a way of showing how pagans, and the Jewish people, were ignorant and blind to the true Messiah. According to the New Testament scripture, such people were hidden from the light, with St Paul declaring in II Corinthians:

> *But if our gospel be hidden, it is hid to them that are lost; In whom the God of this world hath blinded the minds of them which believe not, lest the light of the glorious gospel of Christ, who is the image of God, shine upon them.*

Away from the Bible, theologians declared blindness as a form of mental disturbance – a person who was '*caecus*', 'aimless and confused', and a state set outside the earthly experience. St Ambrose, the fourth-century commentator and Bishop of Milan, referred to blindness as 'passion' and 'madness'. St Jerome, of the same period, points to it as a form of 'arrogance'.

Similar texts report not only upon the blind as 'incomplete' – their bodies representative of their souls and even immoral – but worse, often as a stereotype to be mocked. The greatest church father of them all, St Augustine, wrote in his famed *City of God* that blindness caused 'furore and dementia'. To lose one's sight was to lose one's mind. Psychiatrists would take up this theme again in the early twentieth century, and the description was often applied to soldiers returning from the First World War, blinded by shellshock and trauma.

Such notions of blindness were anything but cheery reading, as it told me yet again the perpetual backdrop to being blind is about being defined with a separate, different identity; one that is usually full of tragedy and foreboding. My reading certainly helped me to understand why blind people were and are still pitied, and why the Swedish nuns, the Scottish journalist in Rome, and people who tilt their heads and pray for me are merely tapping into a millennia-old template of sightlessness. If the Bible and the images from its stories tell us it is natural to pity or fear those individuals who are blind, and this notion has been handed down from century to century, it surely means I must – or at least attempt to – forgive those in society who know no better.

*   *   *

One adventure in the Holy City that completely disrupted my notions of these binary interpretations of blindness arrived during my last weeks in Rome as, after four years, I had decided to head back to the UK and start a new job.

As I have said, my time in Rome was a delight, and during my first year I made the rather eccentric decision to learn Latin – because that is what you do when in Rome. A dear friend introduced me to Father Reginald Foster at the Vatican – or 'Reggie', as he was widely known. He was the best scholar in town, she said, and he will make you roar with laughter and speak Latin. When he wasn't programming, in Latin, the Vatican ATM or writing encyclicals for the Pope (he was the foreign secretary to the Vatican), Reggie gave his time to teach free Latin lessons for the *'ignoramus'*. These lessons were sometimes held in ancient school rooms at his university, or *'sub-aboribus'* at his Carmelite monastery up on San Pancrazio – a hill just outside Rome. Reggie deeply believed that the study of languages – their construction, their meaning and tone – was the basis of all human knowledge. He also believed all this knowledge was best swallowed with bad, tepid white wine, which he bought by the flagon and insisted we drink to help us to become more loquacious with our Latin.

Sadly, my Latin, and attendance at his classes – or experiences, as he called them – were terrible, but somehow Reggie and I became *Amici Mirabelle* (best friends). Dressed in his blue jeans and plumber's jacket (much to the Church's chagrin, Reggie refused to wear clerical dress), he would greet me in Latin: '*Cur tarde Venis Monocular?*' (*Why are you late, one eyed one?*) as I came into class; '*Allium Spiritus Relinquo!*' (*Avoiding garlic!*) I would retort, as Reggie reeked of the stuff – he told us he ate raw garlic at three o'clock every morning to keep him healthy.

One of the most memorable moments with Reggie in Rome was, it turns out, one of my last times with him. I was about to head back to England to start a new job and attend the dinner where I would hear about Nandy the Neanderthal. With garlic breath and all, he demanded I meet him at eight a.m. sharp at St Anne's Gate of the Vatican. Other friends had told me that, as a parting gift from the city, he would often show departing students the Sistine Chapel before the touristic hoards charged in, so I eagerly agreed.

Meeting me at the precise hour, with two Swiss Guards protecting the threshold of the tiny city-state, he roared his usual welcome of '*Monoculaaaar!*' so all could hear and marched me up some steps. He took me through silent marble corridors, with scarlet-clad cardinals floating past, then charged up narrow stairs which circled up like a double helix and passed frescos of birds perched on climbing flowers. (Here he gave me the history of the word 'grotesque', which pertains to the paintings done in the grottos.) Suddenly, without warning, he landed us at an innocuous blank wooden door. 'That's the Sistine Chapel,' he pointed, 'but we don't have time today. Another time!' and with a deep grunt, he charged past and led me down yet more corridors and stairs.

Finally, almost breathless from keeping up with him, I landed at another, slightly larger, inconspicuous door. We entered and I found myself in the hallowed chambers of the *Bibliotequa Apostolica Vaticana* (Vatican library). Even at this early hour, the rooms were full of heads bowed over wooden desks, peering over documents and books. After walking through arcades of shelves, Reggie pulled up a small chair, which could hardly take his robust figure, and sat down, thanking a rather flustered monk for his help. He waved the monk away, and then gestured his hand over a parchment that was laid out. '*Lire!* Read!' he roared. I peered.

He explained: 'It's a seventeenth-century Vatican Commentary on the Decretals of Gregory IX, from circa 1621. It is by the blind Italian writer Doctor Prospero Fagnani. Doctor Caecus Oculatissimus – the blind, yet most far-sighted doctor.' I nodded appreciatively but had no clue. As my Latin really is bad, at the start of this passage is Reginald's translation.

> *The blind, orphans, widows and the aged are to be classified as 'miserable' persons ... from them the Church expects nothing. They need not pay taxes, not make a contribution to the church. This does not mean to imply blindness indicates mental disturbance, for it holds that the blind in mind are to be more pitied than the blind in eye.*

To be honest, at the time I was more impressed I was standing in the Vatican library than reading some ancient parchment (just think *The Da Vinci Code* with a garlic-breath Tom Hanks as hero). I did not really register what Reggie was showing me. He roared in his native Milwaukee twang, 'Don't you see? HA! He is the blind, yet most far-sighted doctor! Get it? Get it?' and smiled with glee.

Perhaps as most people would, I clocked and sighed how the doctor's canonical text reiterated how blindness (and other disabilities) had long been understood as a state of loss and an impairment that was negative. The language shows how Renaissance society accepted how blind people's state of not seeing was considered differently from sighted people: they lived in a separate world, beyond ordinary humankind. The interpretation also seemed to ratify to the

Catholic community how the world of blind people could be infused with a spirituality that gave a peculiar innocence of mind. The doctor is 'Doctor Caecus Oculatissimus – the blind, yet most far-sighted doctor', reminding us, as in the myths of ancient times, that to be blind and clever must mean there is something exceptional about this person. He showed me, too, that blind people, then as now, are presumed to be absent from truth – at least according to the Western tradition – and thus prevented from contributing to society. For millennia, humans have had the need to use blindness as an opposition to something: good versus bad, truth versus lies, black versus white, up versus down. In all these binary oppositions, blindness has come out as a negative, equal to darkness and ignorance.

I did not have much time to digest such thoughts, as within a few minutes of showing me the text Reginald threw himself upwards off the chair and almost dragged me out of a side door. Soon, panting and hurrying (Reggie had to get to work), we were climbing another long marble staircase into an extraordinary gallery covered in ancient pale green world maps. Then through another corridor, down another banal staircase, and boom! without a word, he threw me back into the heat and pollution of St Peter's Square, the morning sunlight beginning to warm the cream Bernini pillars that embrace visitors as they arrive.

We parted, knowing I was leaving Rome the following month. Happily, he did take me to the Sistine Chapel and audio described the ceiling. I will never forget the moment when he yelled, 'Everyone looks at the Creation, but just look at Noah and the Whale!' We then moved back to our separate lives and homes – he to Milwaukee to retire to his Carmelite monastery and I to London. We did, however, stay in regular correspondence, written in his multi-coloured pens, chiding me on my terrible Latin, and always beginning *Salve Monocular!* He even did some Latin lessons (*Ludo*) on YouTube, which were not as good as seeing him live, but give a sense of his teaching methods. He died in 2021 from old age. I feel honoured to have known and been taught by Reginaldis. *Requiescat in pace*, as they say in Rome.

Twenty-five years after leaving the Holy City and the unpitying Reggie, it seems to me, on reflection, that he showed me much more than simply an old manuscript by a blind doctor. Reggie admired and honoured the doctor for his brains, not his lack of sight. Blindness was, for my mad, garlic-smelling priest, a physical state that did not detract or denounce a person; they were simply in a state of not seeing. He also showed me that, despite the whole city bulging with pity, there were people who decided their own terms of engagement and did not have to treat blind people as cases to be pitied, even in the past. In a sense, he gave me the gift of ownership; blind or not, I was in charge of living my own life.

And yet, to know that blindness is endlessly attached to pity, to ignorance, misery and catastrophe, and usually economic disadvantage, is not easy. To understand is one thing. To live with it day-to-day and to be treated accordingly is another. It is something I have not become used to, nor perhaps will I.

* * *

Then he touched their eyes, saying, according to your faith be it unto you, And their eyes were opened.

MATTHEW 10.29–30 (KJV)

As Reggie showed me, blindness was not all gloom and doom, and the idea of not seeing was not always a negative condition in the Christian tradition.

Away from the Canonical texts in the Vatican library, sometimes blindness could also be a useful conduit through which Jesus could prove his power on earth. As the Christian faith and its doctrine and liturgy became more formalized in the twelfth and thirteenth centuries, it also allowed the idea of blindness to have the wonderful potential to be a useful PR tool; it was the perfect way Christians could demonstrate their faith.

Key to this shift in understanding about blindness from classical and biblical times was the idea that owning blindness was through no fault of a person's own actions or behaviour. This was in sharp contrast to the fixed understanding that man's blindness was an irreversible part of his fate. Tiresias could do nothing to change his condition, despite his own mother begging the gods to intervene. Jesus, on the other hand, could change a man's condition with just a word.

In the Gospel of St John, for example, Jesus is walking along the road and meets, we are told, a man who has been without sight since birth. His disciples, whose notions of blindness have been shaped by the Old Testament readings, ask him who had sinned: the blind man or his parents? Jesus is clear it is no one's fault, least of all the blind man:

> *Jesus answered, neither hath this man sinned, nor his parents: but that the works of God should be made manifest in him. I must work the works of him that sent me, while it is day: the night cometh, when no man can work. As long as I am in the world, I am the light of the world.*[1]

---

[1] John 9.3, King James version: William Collins (1957) edition.

Intriguingly, there is no back story that explains why 'this man' is blind (such as Tiresias spying on Athena in the bath) or what he might have done to become blind; he simply is blind. While other stories in the Bible could interpret blindness as an expression of a sinful spirit or soul, Jesus' interpretation shifted the understanding into a neutral state: to be blind was an impairment which God's son could cure.

Again, in the Gospel according to Mark, Jesus says to the blind man, 'Go thy way, thy faith has made thee whole'; the man gets up and is cured. In another rendition in Matthew, Christ cures two blind men by touching their eyes. In John, Jesus applies a compact of spittle and clay to the blind man's eyes and heals him. Repeatedly, the image of Christ healing the sick, lame and blind was part of Christ's ministry on earth; restoration of sight by God's son on earth was depicted in religious paintings, illuminations, art and gravestones, even from the early days of Christianity. At the fourth-century Catacombs of Domitilla in Rome, archaeologists found a sarcophagus with a simple image on the front: a man kneels before Christ, and Christ places a hand on his eyes. Such images frequently appeared in the front portals of churches, as porticos were where the congregation metaphorically stepped from the darkness into light.

As Christianity grew, blindness became an essential linchpin through which the Church could gain a new currency and exert its power. Like Jesus himself, the Church and its operatives aimed to be man's metaphorical spiritual guide, leading the blind man to the light of God and his son's forgiveness. Simply becoming a Christian, via baptism, reflected the true shift from darkness to light. An early convert to Christianity, Tertullian, explains that baptismal water washes away 'the faults of the former blindness' and makes us free for the eternal life.

Indeed, after baptism, the curing of blindness became a key indicator of a person's spiritual health and how Jesus Christ's influence could cure and heal. 'I am the light of the World', Jesus says in the Gospel of John. 'Whosoever follows me will not walk in darkness but will have the light of life.'[2] We are repeatedly told Jesus cured the physically impaired (and specifically the blind) because the curing of them was a manifestation of God's work.

* * *

In some ways I rather enjoyed the use of blindness as a fixing biblical metaphor because it allowed blind people to be shown the transformative power of prayer and faith. In

---

[2] John 9.3, King James version: William Collins (1957) edition.

the sixth-century Italian Codex of Rossano, for example, Christ is seen touching the eye of a blind man, as referred to in the Gospel of John. By believing in the new saviour and his church, the man moved from death (blindness) to salvation (sight). Similar images appear in narrative texts; sixth-century manuscripts from Syria show illuminated images of Christ healing two blind people at the same time.

It was fun to know, too, that the notion of God curing the blind was not entirely new and was mentioned in quite a few other historical texts. Gaius Cornelius Tacitus (56–120 AD), one of the greatest Roman historians, reports that King Vespasian healed a man with his spittle, and all were amazed. Similar stories emerge in texts such as the *Book of Tobit* and the *Letter of Jeremiah*. Many scholars also point out how, in Isaiah, curing blindness was the pinnacle miracle, and a sure sign God was coming to save you: 'And then shall the eyes of the blind be opened' – a refrain taken from Isaiah 35 that would be heard set to music five hundred years later in Handel's glorious oratorio *Messiah*. In the New Testament, the curing of blindness was now witnessed, in real time.

What was appealing about these miracle stories was they happened on earth – not away from the crowd, on some lofty plane or mountain, or reported after the event by a seer. Now, miracles were done for all to see, and blind people were cured by one man – Jesus – and his word alone.

*   *   *

The men travelling with Saul stood there speechless; they heard the sound but did not see anyone. Saul got up from the ground, but when he opened his eyes, he could see nothing. So, they led him by the hand into Damascus. For three days he was blind and did not eat or drink anything.[3]

Perhaps the most well-known Christian story of transformation from darkness to light (and faith) and its impact is the conversion of Saul to Paul. In this most dramatic of stories, Paul finally understands Jesus is his saviour. And yet while these stark binary oppositions were repeatedly imprinted, there was also at least one stark difference from antiquity – for Christians, blindness was *not* the result of sin or past misdeeds (although these interpretations persisted) but simply a state that could show the power of God and his son Jesus Christ.

Retold three times, predominantly in the Acts of the Apostles, we are told about Saul, a fervent and brutal oppressor of Christians, on his way to Damascus with his Christian-persecuting followers. As he walks, a great

---

[3] Acts of the Apostles 9.22–26 King James version: William Collins (1957) edition.

light falls around him, and he falls to the ground in shock and awe. A voice, which declares upon asking that it is Jesus, demands to know why Saul is persecuting the faithful. Importantly, no other companions are blinded, though in some versions of the story not all of them see the light or hear the voice; however, all are aware that something dramatic and powerful has occurred. After three days of blindness, Saul rises from his bed, is baptized in the new faith, regains his sight, and is reborn as Paul. He then goes out to spread the faith – a founding father of the Church and an evangelical apostle. His blindness was not a punishment, but rather a means for him and the witnesses (us and his companions) to see the transformation of an individual to Christianity. We as witnesses, along with Saul, get to see the sharp contrast between before and after the blindness.

By the mid-twelfth century, when Christianity's liturgical engine was in full drive – running the structure of daily lives and considered the true path to eternal life – the concept of blindness had moved away from being viewed as a fixed, unchangeable state, attached only to punishment and sin, to an almost sacred condition which had the possibility of transforming an individual's life. A person could even be temporarily blind and then regain vision, thus showing a true sign of change.

In one way, I must admit to finding the stories of Jesus and his acolytes often very moving. How amazing to have the gift to change someone's life in an instant, and how relieving to know that blindness was not the fault of one's parents, despite our need, these days, to blame them for everything. Blindness, the New Testament tells us, was a state that represented ignorance, and one that could reveal the truth. While this seemed to have very little to do with my own life, it explained the mythology the nuns and priests I met in Rome bought into, not to mention the mad Scottish journalist who wept with pity.

As always, however, the wave of good feeling somehow clashes with one's own reality. What if you are not a saint? Not miraculously cured? Where does that leave you, metaphorically and in actuality? Are you unloved, uncared for and invisible? Or an object of pity, due only charitable actions and the Pity Fest?

*   *   *

Amongst all the blind men being cured, I did wonder: where were the blind women and what role did they play? After not too much searching, I found that parallel to the male-dominated world of parables, priests and popes, and curing miracles revealed in the Bible, early Christian daily life was brimming with the lives of female saints and holy nuns.

While there are literally hundreds of blind saints to choose from in the Christian canon (and we must include the Byzantine saints as well), amongst all the stories, I was most drawn to that of St Lucy of Syracuse, Sicily, the Christian martyr who lived between 283 and 304 AD, who is known to this day as the patron saint of light and eyesight. Mentioned by Dante, Donne and Milton, St Lucy is still venerated across the globe, usually portrayed standing regally with her eyeballs in an open Bible. Her saint's day is on 13 December, which had previously been the feast of the Winter Solstice. Her name, derived from *Lux* – light in Latin – not only referred to her inner truth, but the light she could offer the world.

St Lucy's canonization is the story of a courageous woman; she turned down a suitor, based on her new Christian belief, and died for it. She disobeyed her family and refused to marry, and in the brief life that was left to her, she remained adamant her God was the right God. She did not give in. The rejected suitor reported her to the non-believing local governor, who in turn offered her a few ways out: swearing allegiance to Rome or offering a few sacrifices to the gods, both of which she refused. She chose death and was executed in 304 AD, only a few years before Emperor Constantine converted to Christianity. In later medieval versions, the local governor removes her eyes as she claims to foresee the downfall of the Roman Emperor, Diocletian. In more disturbing narratives, it is said she took out her eyes herself. When she was being prepared for burial in the family plot, her maidservants discovered her eyes were back in place.

As I read her story, I began to like the idea that a blind woman is a model to which we can aspire. She is an example of a life that can be motivating and help us, particularly if we are Catholic, to identify with the qualities of a particular life. We can pray to someone who knows our exact problems and challenges – akin to group therapy today. The blinding of St Lucy shows, like her male counterparts who see the light, that she does not need her eyes to see the inner truth with her genuine holy nature, and courage comes in many forms.

* * *

Lesser-known medieval blind nuns had a slightly different take on how to handle blindness. Take St Odile of Alsace, for example. Her life story is so complicated it would take three volumes to cover it, and I must confess St Odile has become one of my latest pin-up heroines. What a lass! She travelled, she had people read to her, she loved her family despite them treating her badly, and had a wonderful cohort of nuns to support her. Even in death, she gave hope to thousands around Europe – a sort of medieval Helen Keller.

The nub of St Odile's story is that she spends most of her life charging around mountain and vale, transforming, converting, and losing and regaining her sight. Born blind in 660 AD, our young heroine is abandoned to the Church by her father, who wants nothing to do with his blind daughter. Legend tells us that aged twelve she was left at the local monastery, where the local bishop baptised her Odile and she miraculously recovered her sight. This was miracle number one.

The story is then one of epic adventure. When Odile's younger brother, Hugh, hears of his sister's transformation, he goes to find her and returns home with her. Their father, still intransigent, is so angry his instructions have been defied that he kills his son in a fit of rage. In fear for her life, Odile flees across the Rhine valley to Freiburg in Germany (or, in other versions, to Basel in Switzerland). Her father then pursues her, but the local mountain opens miraculously to hide her, and she finds shelter. This is miracle number two. Her father, exhausted, gives up his search, and as he returns home, having been hit by falling stones and struggling through dangerous waterfalls, swears never to see or speak to his daughter again.

As Odile's father becomes ill (and dare we mention, losing his sight) in old age, he yields to his fiery daughter's conversion, and allows her to attend to him. Indeed, with his blessing and help, they found the Augustine monastic community of Mont St Odile, now known as Hohenburg Abbey, in the Bas-Rhin. Odile becomes its Abbess, and her father lives with her and remains under her care. After he dies, and following a vision of St John the Baptist, Odile founds a second monastery and hospital, specifically dedicated to help those with blindness and eye ailments.

Finally, in 720 AD (aged 60) Odile dies, but is again revived by the prayers of her sisters at the convent (miracle number three). Alive again, she describes the beauties of the afterlife and takes communion, but sadly dies again; she is buried alongside her beloved and forgiven father and raised to sainthood within a hundred years of her life, with her name and fame becoming pan-European. Chapels, churches and monasteries were all consecrated to her honour, and pilgrimages to her grave were very popular for the masses.

While one can only admire Odile, and others such as St Margaret of Metola or St Cecilia, I found myself considering that not only did they have horrible deaths, so their blindness did not really help them, but also that I did not want to aspire to being perfect. What about having a bad day? Slurping your soup, or bumping into a lamppost? Even treading in dog poo? Odile's life is not very real. Yet her life made me understand that the connection between blindness, ignorance and darkness was pervasive and tightly bound into the whole myth of blindness. The only reason it evokes pity is because sighted people imagine it to be worse than death, and thus feel pity – charity – for those afflicted. It is a model often referred to by academics as the Charity model – and it is not one I find very comfortable.

* * *

I began this chapter thinking about how darkness has been heavily aligned to not seeing. Partway through my career, I met Father Reggie, and I learnt that blindness is not the identity every blind person has to adopt. Then I heard about Nandy the Neanderthal and decided to delve further and write a book. But one day, having relinquished my dance with the blind nuns and saints, I found myself having a night off, and watching one of those wonderful nature documentaries where you can't remember the name of any of the species or fauna.

For a while, I was transfixed by the hundreds of beings deep beneath the waters, where species not only thrive in the darkness but reject the light. Did you know, for example, there are anglerfish which have giant heads, sharp teeth and a big mouth like a fishing pole, with bioluminescent bacteria that attract prey? These live perfectly happily in the deeps, at 40, even 50 metres below the surface.

Such creatures living quite happily in darkness reminded me how darkness is not all dark, and some medieval theologians and thinkers came to be more nuanced about God and darkness. Indeed, medieval scholar Hermes Trismegistus argued in his *Corpus Hermeticum* that the light of God could be almost blinding: 'You have filled us with vision, and my mind's eye is almost blinded in such a vision.' In the same way, people retrospectively attributed more darkness-banishing miracles to Jesus; the Bible also offered treasures that showed us all that darkness was not always obscure and deathly, but could be useful in our path towards God. One well-known passage from St Paul's Epistle to the Corinthians is quoted frequently as proof of the very ambiguity of light and darkness: 'For now, we see through a glass, darkly; but then face to face: now I know in part; but then shall I know even as also I am known.'[4] I am not sure if blindness has ever helped me find God, but as I watched the strange deep-sea fish, it was nice to know that sight and light are not always known in a binary fashion. Sometimes things are complicated.

Even now, as I lose what remains of my sight, I know that while my working eye sees misty fog and shadows of vision,

---

[4] St Paul's Epistle to the Corinthians 12, King James Version, William Collins (1957) edition.

my blind right eye does not see black or dark, but simply does not see. A quick chat with blind friends informs me that they experience the same; while blindness for them is not seeing, rather than a black sheet of velvet, for sighted people, the presumption is always the latter.

And yet, despite this factual knowledge, our modern-day notion of blindness is still attached and perpetuates the binary opposition which shows that darkness and blindness go hand in hand, which in turn leads to blind people being perceived as non-functioning objects of pity and burdens on society. While there has always been a need for humans to marginalize, objectify and stigmatize those groups of people they fear or don't like, this can go to the extreme of excluding any groups you don't think are viable, whether blind or not.

As my grandmother would say, it's an unpleasant thought, but still part of humanity.

3

Faking it

False eyes, false sight, and the Devil

When I left Rome and headed back to London, I realized my sight was heading towards blindness a little more every day, month and year.

But while I understood this intellectually, I remained a little bit more in denial than I should have. The loss of my sight was not so daunting (so I thought) because I could carry on in my journalism career and did so with optimism at the *Daily Telegraph* and BBC Radio. This floaty sense of not really engaging with the reality of my life was cut short a few times when people – ignorant people – accused me of being a malingerer, a faker or a fraud.

The most shocking accusation of 'faking' came after a train journey from Scotland. Arriving at King's Cross, I tapped my way to the barrier with my cane and hung it on my arm in order get my ticket out of my wallet. I stepped up to the gate and the guard stopped me. 'Can I see your ticket?' he asked. I duly supplied it. 'Can I see your disabled travel card please?' I pulled it out, knowing as I did that it was in a certain compartment of my wallet. 'How did you get that then?' Get what? 'Your disability travel card? I mean, you can see all right, can't you?'

Having learnt to be patient with other non-believers, I was calm. 'Oh, I know, but I have only got about 20 per cent vision on a good day. The doctors tested me ...' Unconvinced, the guard continued: 'You think you can get your card, and just get away with it. I saw you walking down the platform, bright and breezy. You are faking it!' He was quite proud of his little diatribe and did not seem keen to let me through unless I confessed to my high crimes and misdemeanours. My brain fizzed, and having been the calm and graceful person I would like to be, a surge of anger overwhelmed me and I just lost it. I shouted and waved my arms about in rage, my cane flailing on its strap on my wrist, possibly hitting passengers alongside me. 'Excuse me?' The queue behind me was beginning to build up. One man said, 'Oh come on. Just let her through.'

But my stress levels were too high. 'I'll tell you what is fake ... My eye – my hand-painted false eye. Here! Let me show you!' With great panache I ripped out my false eye, put it in my palm and offered it forward. The queue gasped. I was shaking with fury. 'You really think I had my real eye plucked out and went through the pain of having a false eye made, just to get a discount on my f**king train ticket?' The guard was mortified. 'I am sorry, sorry ... er ... look do you need any help going through ... I didn't realize.' I went berserk: 'You stay away from me, you vile man.'

Incandescent with rage, I placed my beautiful hand-painted eye in my pocket, unfurled my white cane and marched off. I walked over to the nearby coffee shop and sat down shaking, waiting for about 30 minutes to recover myself. It took me a day to have enough equilibrium to report the guard (I had the time and date, and, apparently, all the gates have cameras on them) and received a mighty apology from the train company, with a promise that the guard would undergo serious training and possibly suspension. To be honest, I didn't care what they did, as I just wanted to move on from the episode. But to this day, I shudder at the memory and wonder how many other people the train guard had accused of fakery. I doubt he will again.

*   *   *

Perhaps my sense of outrage was because I had been born blind in my right eye – a defect at birth, our doctors told us – and thus had grown up with a beautiful, hand-painted Perspex false eye, which I put in every morning. Because of this, my face looks what is commonly known as 'normal'.

While my plastic eye has remained a constant, my remaining sight has diminished.

My parents first took me to a 'false eye maker' when I was around ten. It was quite an adventure as I had to take a day off school, and my mother explained that after visiting the new 'eye' doctor we would pay a visit to my favourite hamburger joint, the Hard Rock Café – the place for birthdays or excellent school reports, neither of which were due or had been achieved. Rising early, we went to a large building, pressed on a huge circular brass button, and then struggled into an old rickety lift, which did not stop level at each floor. As we arrived to the third floor, a short blonde woman, with puce coral lipstick and a soothing low voice, pulled the gate back and welcomed us.

She was very calm and gentle. Putting her hand out to meet me, she smiled and then crouched down on her haunches, leant forward and peered at me. Her name was Paula, she said, and she was going to take a good long look at my eyes. She said, 'You have a beautiful hazel in your eye. It will be fun to match that.' It was the first time I ever knew I had hazel eyes, despite having stared at myself in the mirror for hours. I could not, and still can't, see myself very clearly.

She then took me by the hand into an almost empty room and sat me in a black barber-like chair with a headrest which tilted backwards. As if from nowhere, she brought around a tray covered with a white cloth. 'Now,' she cooed, 'don't be frightened. I want to show you what we are going to make you today.' She waved her hand across the tray, like an air hostess serving a beverage, and removed the cloth. Beneath were rows and rows of false eyes staring blankly up at me, lined up like hardboiled sweets or spawn. Each one was unique, and I was beguiled by the array of colours, shades, and daintily painted blood vessels and pupils. Somehow, I did not feel the absurdity or weirdness of the situation; it was like going to a smart jeweller and having a tray of rings or brooches presented to you. One simply had to choose.

Paula (as I was to call her for years) then went on to explain how she made the eyes: 'We take a mould from your non-working eye socket and fill it with liquid plastic. That then hardens – and I take it away for a few weeks to paint it.' She then pointed to a Polaroid camera. 'I take a picture of your good eye and copy it almost exactly – never completely, as no two eyes look the same. It will look like one of these eyes but be just for you.' She smiled encouragingly, and then explained she would make me three eyes – one for the daytime, one for the night-time when your pupils dilate, and an extra one for emergencies. Three eyes? Emergencies? It was akin to choosing shoes or a handbag for spring or summer – an eye for all seasons.

As an adult, I have even been tempted to have a 'party' eye – with an exclamation mark or a target painted in the centre – but I have yet to find the courage.

And so we began, my mother standing behind the chair, asking all sorts of annoying practical questions as mothers tend to do – about how to keep it, and whether washing-up liquid was a good detergent for washing 'it'. Despite Paula's calm, reassuring voice and the gentleness of her manner, the process was painful. With my head at a 90-degree angle facing upwards, I had to wait in the same position for about 20 minutes while she poured blue goo into my eye socket and waited for it to set. It stung greatly, and my neck throbbed and ached from being fixed for so long.

After a while I wanted to cry, but Paula's coral lips persuaded me kindly not to because it would mean we would have to go through the entire process again. I remember being rigid with fear as the goo hardened around my real eyeball, and how she had to almost wrench it out in one piece. It felt as if my optic nerve was being pulled out from the back of my head. A small consolation for the pain was that we very rarely had to redo the 'blue goo' process, because she would widen and lengthen the original template as I grew up.

Perhaps because I was so young when I started acquiring false eyes, I didn't question having them; it seemed part of the medical rounds we took over the years. My parents explained that they wanted me to have 'every opportunity' of my sighted contemporaries; having a false eye, I would appear 'normal'. They wanted me judged on my abilities, not my disabilities. Their view was not unusual or uncommon, and echoed that of Franklin D. Roosevelt, who always had photos taken of himself from the waist up to hide his wheelchair because he feared people would not take him seriously if he was seen as disabled. Interestingly, the next president, Lyndon Johnson, felt differently, pulling up his shirt on many occasions to show his scars from war as proof of his strength. As a child and a young adult, I did not question it, and I would hop off to the 'eye maker' to get a replacement when my face grew. I considered it simply part of my life, like getting a haircut or going to the dentist. It was not a false eye, but *my* eye – part of me, freckles and all.

So if you are blind or visually impaired, when do you fake seeing or not fake it? Before I got married and was on the dating circuit, I often wondered when I should tell my dates about my eyesight. Before the first date? During the first date? Or five weeks later? When is it okay to reveal you simply can't see that much? Sometimes I joked with it: 'Just to say I am visually impaired, but don't worry, this means I will imagine you are very handsome and very fit,' which worked occasionally, particularly with older gentlemen. But I also recall going on a second date and the fellow asked me if I was already drunk, simply because I fell over a lot in the park. When I told him I could not see, except for blur, he accused me of making it up: 'But you can see something, non?'

Interestingly, I felt so comfortable with my now beloved husband, I told him about my sight or lack of straight away, before our first date, and he reacted in his usual philosophical way: 'Oh, that's interesting. Quite a few important philosophers have considered the nature and importance of blindness, you know. Let me get you a paper on the Molyneux problem.' And off he toddled, coming back with a long eighteenth-century philosophy tract about the nature of sight.

He even bought me, along with flowers, translations of Denis Diderot's *Lettre sur les aveugles à l'usage de ceux qui voient*, published in England in 1770 as *Letter on the Blind for the Use of Those Who Can See*. The letter is often cited as proof that Diderot dismissed intelligent design and all notions of God. The government of the day felt it so subversive that he was arrested and imprisoned for three months after its publication. But as a first gift to a new girlfriend, it showed me how my suitor (and now husband) understood, in a predominantly sighted world, how a blind person could have a rich interior life, with their own agency.

Thank God for academics.

* * *

Not everyone is as enlightened as my husband. As I write, you will be surprised to learn that even now there is a great debate raging on social media about the famed blind, deaf author and disability advocate Helen Keller, and whether she faked her blindness or not.[1]

Helen's basic biography is quite well known, particularly in the United States, where her story was told endlessly in the play, and subsequently film, *The Miracle Worker*, staring Patti Duke and Anne Bancroft (1962). Born in 1880 in Tuscumbia, Alabama, Helen became deaf, blind and non-speaking (known as 'dumb' at the time) after a serious childhood illness. Helen's story is that of a badly behaved, blind, deaf and non-speaking child, who had temper tantrums and whose parents despaired, but then became, with the help of her faithful teacher, a forceful woman who travelled the world and inspired millions with her belief that disability should not stop her, or others, living their lives. With the help of her 'teacher', Annie Sullivan, Helen learnt to speak her first word, '*WaWa*' for 'water', as she ran her hands over a water pump in her garden. From water, she progressed to the alphabet, books and writing; by the time she was

---

[1] https://time.com/5918660/helen-keller-disability-history/. See also: Was Helen Keller a fraud?: r/conspiracy (reddit.com).

twenty-three, she had attended high school and she graduated from Radcliffe College (now Harvard University) and become an established and deeply respected author and memoir writer.

Once she was a fully-fledged adult, Helen worked tirelessly for the American Foundation for the Blind (AFB) from 1924 until 1968, during which time she toured the United States and travelled to 39 countries around the globe advocating on behalf of blind and visually impaired people. At first, I rather liked her gumption, and while her chirpy, cheery narrative slightly disturbed me – did she ever have a bad day? – behind the saintliness she was what we might call in modern terms a 'disruptive' woman.

Despite these very well known, checked and evidence-based facts, a whole new generation on social media have claimed she lied about how disabled she was. In a now-deleted tweet, a young woman said she was a 'Helen Keller denier' because she and her generation had the right to challenge the myth and icon of disability. Over 600,000 people shared the 'Helen Keller is a fraud' social media note (on Redditt and Twitter), and debates thunder on. Really? Is it so hard to believe that a deaf-blind woman could achieve so much? Despite not always liking the Helen Keller myth, it is shocking people deny her disabilities.

So where, as a woman irreversibly losing her sight, and with her hand-painted false eye, do I fit in this twenty-first-century world, which relies on vision, and at the same time relies on proof of blindness? Am I a blind woman, or a visually impaired woman? By wearing a false eye, am I perpetuating a 'fraudulent' image of myself and pandering to the need to fit in? When is it useful to declare one's visual impairment or blindness? And when is it useful to hide it, and fake seeing? And is there any reason that sighted people don't want to recognize and acknowledge blindness as simply blindness?

As I was to discover, the devil is in the detail.

* * *

While we could pick any era in the past five thousand years to look at how blindness has been attached as a symbol for deception and fraud, one of the most exaggerated notions of the 'untrustworthy' and 'fake' blind person occurs in the mid-to-late Middle Ages, when Christianity and the Catholic Church held full sway over people's daily lives. While it might seem far-fetched to compare the meanness and attempted humiliation of one unfriendly guard at King's Cross, or the Helen Keller deniers, with the brush of late medieval superstition and Christian fear, surprisingly there are many echoes.

For a start, the meaning of blindness in medieval times held many associations. The Middle English adjective used to describe blindness, '*blynd*', designated a range of physical meanings: from a temporary or permanent visual impairment to a complete lack of sight. And in a metaphorical sense, 'blind' also suggested deep negative connotations, such as being spiritually unaware or being deluded, mistaken, deceived or sometimes just plain evil. Worse still, such an understanding was validated by the language used by the educated elite, Latin, where the adjective '*caecus*' meant 'blind man' (person with no sight) but was mainly used to suggest negative traits like 'aimless', 'confused', 'random' or 'rash'. More broadly, it could also mean 'dark, hidden and secret'. Heaven help you if you were not a saint, a prince, or the subject of a miracle in medieval Europe.

Part of the stigma around blindness was inherited from the classical era, where the gods had predestined each person with their fate – which, if it involved wrongdoing, would lead to punishment and suffering. Similarly, in the Middle Ages, each community had to decide how and why people in their group were different and should be made outliers. Stigma, as the great sociologist Erving Goffman wrote in 1963,[2] is one of the clear ways a society creates its social divisions and social hierarchies. Medieval

---

[2] Goffman, Erving, *Stigma* (Penguin, 1963).

blindness, therefore, was used to separate 'the blind' by being abandoned, itinerant and poor.

To the medieval mind, therefore, blindness showed the 'incomplete' body, and thus an absence of something. Such 'absence' was a good medium through which to prove difference, particularly for the Church, and could be used to show (for his followers) Jesus' ability to be a miraculous healer and a spiritual physician, and in turn to ask for alms and charity. The early Catholic Church therefore 'needed' people with impairments, of every kind, to ratify an earthly economy; through salvation and redemption, a community or individual could give charity and alms to save those considered the bottom of the economy.

For the majority, other than those cured by miracles, blindness was a sign of sin – either by the owner of the blindness, or their family, or by punishment; some noble or community power could inflict blindness for theft, rape or even adultery. Possibly because of this, blind people were generally mistrusted and surrounded by suspicion. In the medieval mind, I think blind people prompted the question by the sighted faithful: 'What have they done that such a calamity should befall them?'

The medieval mind therefore knew there were individuals who had named 'impairments' and 'misfortunes', which could mean one was lame, blind or deaf, in the same way a person could be labelled 'greedy' or 'a cuckold' or be defined by their profession ('the preacher') or their position in society, such as Chaucer's Wife of Bath. Critically, each impairment had characteristics and stigma attached to it. If blind, for example, but not a visionary or seer, a prophet, a rare subject of Christian healing miracles or even someone with a powerful position, then they were poor, itinerant and lowly outsiders. Blindness was generally understood as a distressing sign of physical disorder and low status. At the elite courts across Europe, in various versions of chess, a blind carved figure on the board was referred to as the 'cunning' one.

There are several rich resources of the late medieval period to delve into, including romances, fables, farces, tapestry and glass illuminations, and if you want even more detailed scholarly knowledge, I would highly recommend the work of scholars such as Irene Metzler and Edward Wheatley. I learnt from my medieval audit that Christians had a very different relationship and understanding of the body and bodily impairments from the one we have now. The word 'disability', for example, which is part of our common parlance, was not used until the late eighteenth and early nineteenth centuries, where one was either 'able' to work or 'not able', and thus was 'disabled'.

In sharp opposition to the Church's ability to offer care and support, perhaps one of the more ominous connections to blindness, and one that was represented across Western Europe, was the association with the Devil – or, as he was more often known, the Antichrist.

What was most frightening about the Devil and all his works was his amazing ability to *fake* being normal. The most obvious example was, of course, in the form of a serpent to Adam and Eve, but further Bible stories also had St Paul warning the Corinthians that the Devil can appear as an 'Angel of Light' or a being that could 'blind you from the truth'. Not only could the Devil be blind or one-eyed, but he also had the power to blind those around him. Thus, blindness was not only indicated by what it could do to the eyes of the Devil, but also that it had the power to blind – a double blinder, if ever there was one.

Indeed, anything that appeared separate and 'other' (as applied to most disabilities) meant a difference that could imply away from the good and true. The Devil's pernicious figure came in many disguises and configurations, but the medieval understanding of him, illiterate or not, would always be that one could recognize his deceptive and hypocritical ways from the posture and shape of his body, his hair and, of course, his eyes.

Most of these images, and thus connections with evil, were made clear in illuminations, windows and tapestries. Some very specific written descriptions gave a clear clue as to how such a blind Devil might look: his right eye, according to the third-century Syriac *Testament of the Lord*, would be shot through with blood, his left eye blue-black with two pupils. These traits would show how impure he was, and how deceptive he was. It did not even matter if he was not completely blind – he might even see with *one* eye – but the fact his sight was disrupted at all meant he was a being of whom we should be wary. This figure could hurt, maim, ruin and destroy anything in his path, and do so with intent and malice, all with the glance of his eye. To be the Devil, in whatever form, would be a person who concealed his real evilness but only gave hints of it in his posture and eyes. In other words, anyone who was blind had the potential to be the Antichrist. Who knew!

To read such stories in modern times made me part-grimace and part-smile. On the one hand, as with classical mythical figures, none of these superstitions really had an impact on me. Here were stories from a thousand years ago, when constructs of society were very different, and notions of evil or even religion shaped our lives far more. Even if not of a religious persuasion, the notion of a single force, a point of evil, did not sit reasonably with me – aside from the baddies in films, my all-round education and culture does not see people in such extreme binary oppositions. I did not want to take the narrative at face value.

At the same time, it is also fair to say that such images quietly amused me and echoed the feelings about being special. In such a society, it appeared that I would be a purveyor of great power, albeit evil power, and I would be seen to have the capacity to ruin people's lives. It also felt as if blindness and blind people were comic – with characterizations everyone would know. How wonderful to be a one-eyed person, with the ability to zap anyone I wished (such as mean and cruel train station guards) and make people run away simply by showing my wandering eye. I am obviously being facetious, but in terms of history, having any status in my blindness, even if evil, was intriguing.

As I let these evil fantasies run around in my head, I found myself wondering why people would be cruel and mean to blind people in the modern day. As I would discover in thirteenth-century French farce, fear and loathing come well into it.

*   *   *

Away from the Devil and all his works, another popular mainstream image of the blind man in the medieval mind, one deeply engrained in the image of evil and blindness, was the concept that ordinary blind people could be entertainment, because they were hoodwinking the world. We know this not just from art, but also from a plethora of medieval ballads, romances, farces, poems, artefacts and fabliaux (bawdy poem plays) which depict a comic representation of the blind man, out to deliberately trick the public.

There are quite a few gruesome examples to choose from, but the most famous tale, written in the thirteenth century and well known across the following two centuries, was entitled *Le Garcon et l'Aveugle* (The Boy and the Blind Man) and first performed in the market square of Tournai, then in France, now a town in Belgium. The story begins with a blind man on stage bemoaning that he doesn't have a guide, which prevents him from moving around to beg for alms. A young boy arrives who offers to be his guide for a small fee. The blind man (note, he has no name) is thrilled, and declares that now they will make more money together, as the boy can sing at the same time as he, the blind man, begs.

The new couple make a deal: the blind man promises the boy a share of the day's takings. However, when they do not do well, the blind man reassures the boy he has a private stash back at his home, saying with glee, 'If I ever stop asking for bread, I will still maintain myself nicely, having amassed so much money.' Things, however, take a rather lewd turn when the young boy, in a bid to cheer them up, offers to fetch a young maiden to have sex with. The blind man dismisses the idea as not only does he already have a girl, but they have such an adventurous time in bed, he can even balance dice on the soles of her feet while making love. The boy protests at such banter and excuses himself for a moment to take a pee. Instead of leaving the stage, however, the boy puts on a fake voice, and returns as a passer-by who begins to berate the blind man for his begging and his sexual perversion. He then slaps and pushes the defenceless blind man about, ripping his clothes and taunting him. Of course, the young boy now 'returns' to rescue his new master and takes him home to recover.

The final showdown ends the play with the lad showing the assumed true stupidity of the blind man. The clever sighted one offers to fix his clothes and get some food if the blind man will supply him with money. Grateful, the blind man hands over clothes and his entire purse, believing still in the goodness of the young boy. Instead, he ends up being rebuked by the boy as he goes: 'Fie on you! Am I not out of your reach? You're nothing but a turd to me. You're the trickster and a jealous person; if it were not for companions (like me) you would be rich by millions, but you will pay for them, and if you aren't satisfied, run after me.' The play ends with the blind man on the stage, naked and alone. Saturday nights in downtown Tournai must have been a quite a riot with the audience roaring with glee at the blind man's downfall.

Another French play also indulged in the pantomime nature of blindness and the stumbling around blind man image. In Paris in 1425, an anonymous chronicler depicted the latest entertainment.

> *On the last Sunday of the month of August there took place an amusement at the residence ... in the rue Saint Honoré in which four blind people all armed, each with a stick, were put in a pen and in that location, there was a strong pig that they could have if they killed it. Thus, it was done, and there was a very strange battle, because they gave themselves so many great blows with those stick that it went worse for them, because when the stronger ones believed that they hit the pig, they hit each other ...*[3]

As the medieval scholar Edward Wheatley points out, this report is shocking in its calculated cruelty. How could we be entertained by blind people killing a pig? For a start, it was expensive (someone had to buy the pig in the first place). Above all, though, it draws a crowd. The chronicler doesn't even worry that the blind men might hurt or damage each other. Even more disturbingly, it is considered by leading historians to be one of the first, if not the first, French farces,

---

[3] Wheatley, Edward. *Stumbling Blocks before the Blind: Medieval Constructions of Blind*ness (University of Michigan Press, 2010), pp. 2–3.

and was popular for centuries.[4] It shows very clearly how a medieval society knew and bought into the assumed identity (stupid) of any blind person, and more than likely used pre-existing stereotypes which were widely understood across the Continent. Blind characters were recognized as greedy, stingy and deserving of being taken advantage of.

These entertainments taught me what historians have called an expression of medieval anxiety: any incompleteness and oddity of the human body had to have a reason, and for the medieval mind this included blindness. Worse still, what really gave extreme distrust to blindness was that the role of the blind man was always played by a sighted person. If you think about it, this implies anyone could feign the impairment. Perhaps we can forgive such cruelty from a group of people whose lives were controlled and negotiated via strict religious rules and theological constructions, including the assumed harsh humiliation of blindness. Isn't it understandable that something you have been told all your life is dangerous and bad provokes fear and loathing?

* * *

One other aspect of medieval history and blindness also stayed with me. As I dived into long volumes in the Bodleian

---

[4]Wheatley, *Stumbling Blocks before the Blind*.

Library at Oxford University, I found many references to the blind beggar. As we saw in classical times, blind beggars, musicians and poets have been familiar figures across Europe for thousands of years, particularly in villages and towns, where blind people were allowed (licensed) to beg, sing and recite poetry at city gates and town halls; they were so well known they often appeared in pictorial and literary representations.

What was noticeable in the medieval period was how the stigma around blindness not only continued, but was amplified. In one well-reported incident in 1390 in France, beggars from Chartres who had been in the company of blind folk drank from a well which subsequently went putrid and poisoned the town. Blindness was obviously to blame. Just being close to blind people could imply or create evil. Blindness was endlessly relied upon as a means to discuss truth and lies, a horrendous trope for Christians to use against Jews for centuries. Depending on the culture, sometimes a blind person was rejected and segregated; sometimes they disappeared without explanation; sometimes they were simply left at the city gates and left to depend on begging.

The image of a blind beggar had deep biblical ramifications, and while there were many different representations of blind people across both Old and New Testaments, one of the images people came to know most was based on lines from Matthew 15.14 in which Jesus is quoted as saying, when referring to unbelievers: 'Let them alone: they be blind leaders of the blind. And if the blind lead the blind, both shall fall into the ditch.' Images based on this Bible verse abound, but perhaps one of the most famous images is by Brueghel the Elder. Entitled *The Blind Leading the Blind*, the painting (currently in the Museo Capodimonte, Naples) famously shows a line of six blind men, each of whom holds onto the man in front of him.

Let me try and offer a verbal description for you. The lead man (at far right) has fallen on the ground; the next is in the process of tripping over him; and the next seems distressed and has realized that his predecessor is falling, and that he too will fall. A friend described to me that the men all wear different outfits, but all have their black shoes and wooden walking sticks, to indicate sightlessness, and they wear loose outer garments (including coats and cloaks) and hose. Blindness was, in the main, depicted as the figure of a poor, gesturing and often simpering person who was helpless and manipulative.

This image of a forlorn, gesturing soul has stayed in our collective imaginations for many centuries. In particular, the late eighteenth- and nineteenth-century 'do-gooders' all indulged in the pitying blind beggar image regularly.

John Thomas Smith's etching of 1816, entitled *Two Blind Beggars*, shows one figure wearing a placard around his neck, with 'BLIND' written on it, and the other with his arms outstretched. The irony, of course, is not lost on the viewer: the blind man cannot even read his own placard, nor have his own voice. According to art historians of the era, it was quite the norm for blind beggars to 'read aloud' stories in a bid to give the impression they were literate, despite their impairments (an aspect of faking sight), hoping to impress passers-by and convince them to give a donation. But it often worked to blind people's disadvantage; many sighted people presumed such acts were fraudulent, and therefore such folk were marginalized and associated in the popular imagination with begging and imitation.

This tradition continued well into the Victorian period, with paintings such as Josephus Laurentius Dyckmans's *The Blind Beggar* (1853) or John Everett Millais's *The Blind Girl* (1856) showing a dishevelled, poor, docile, helpless-looking blind person to evoke emotion, usually pity, and ultimately, one might presume, charity. There are many other paintings of blind beggars and poverty-stricken blind people, but I think this will do for now.

* * *

So have we changed since the Middle Ages?

I am not sure. A few months ago, sneaking a break from my books, I found myself watching a US chat show called *Ellen*. In a bid to boost audience participation, Ellen DeGeneres, the doyenne of afternoon chat, introduced a new game segment to her show, in which the audience could participate and win prizes. The game was called 'Crazy musical chairs!!!!' (her exclamation marks, not mine), which essentially was musical chairs with a twist: six people being blindfolded in 'crazy' blindfolds (which had on their front wide-eyed doll-like eyes) having to find the remaining chairs to sit on when the music stopped.

For approximately five minutes, with funky beat music playing in the background, temporarily blinded folk stumbled around the stage, arms stretched and groping into space. Some fell on the floor, some crawled around – seeking a chair or guidelines of the carpet. Others pulled at each other with undignified excitement, while a few floated around, almost offstage, looking perplexed and bemused with their new status.

At first, the audience sniggered when seats were scrambled over and crashed into. But as the game progressed, they began to cheer loudly at those who wandered offstage or bumped into each other. By the end, when the last two women crawled and wrestled for the last chair, the audience stood up, clapping and roaring with glee. No harm was done, of course. When the participants removed their blindfolds, they stood up, hugged each other, and returned to the world of the sighted with free holidays and new Bluetooth headphones.

We might say this was just another example of the genre of physical theatre that has been entertaining people for centuries, and is now echoed in circuses, pantomimes ... and ailing TV shows. But for me, it was how the audience enjoyed the gesturing and falling over of the blinded (temporarily) participants that seemed disturbing.

Of course, it is clear from the tone of the Ellen DeGeneres show that it was not intended to be cruel or insulting to anyone, let alone blind people, or to remind us of farces and parables from late medieval history. Yet as the audience roared, I thought to myself that, in the fifteenth century, French writers would probably recognize the symbolism of the game. Even though the obvious understanding that blindness is a learnt social construct which distances us, and that behaviour towards blind people is not inherent but acquired via ordinary everyday processes, even now we attack and distance ourselves from what we fear the most, and by watching blind gestures, we still find them funny. Not seeing provides great physical theatre.

After months reading these entertainments, both old and new, I think my horror at their meaning and coding made me realize, in the twenty-first century, my relationship to blindness had become a question of not becoming a victim to the challenges of sight loss, or society's perception of blindness. I do not want to be labelled, judged, or elicit pity. I do not want to be defined only by my blindness.

What I found hard about these brief dips into medieval entertainment, and even the daytime TV show, is the clear objectification and stigma surrounding blindness. Despite the niceties of modern-day liberal thought, it is sad to know there is still such a resistance to the idea that blind people can live and contribute to society in many ways, false eyes or not, and they are not a source of entertainment.

I hate the idea that blindness is a word which implies that blind people are entirely reliant on others – with charities still offering images of poor people from developing countries suffering from blindness, their arms reaching out for help and sustenance.

Dare to be a fluid, functioning, ordinary person who simply gets up, travels on trains, works, has friends, husbands, children, and you threaten the very rigid (and centuries-old) image of how blindness is perceived.

It really beggars belief.

4

Fixing it

The lure of the cure

Surgery has been mooted in the past. I have some reservations about this. She seems to be managing with tasks at present . . . Surgery may be more complex than average, since there may be posterior lenticonus and a central posterior capsular defect. Finally, the rotary nystagmus suggests there may not be foveal fixation in the left eye, which may limit visual benefit.[1]

Newspapers can be nasty things, in more ways than one.

The *Daily Telegraph* office was in the City of London and I commuted there every day, missing my warmer days in Rome, loathing the tube rides, and often spending all my salary on taxis. As a junior member of the team, I was often on weekend duty, and this involved going to the office to

---

[1] Report on eyesight of Selina Mills, 5 September 2018, from leading eye specialist.

follow up on some stories, set up the agenda for the next week, and as usual moaning about the media. One weekend, I turned the page and caught the sharp corner of the paper in my one functioning eye; as it pierced my eye membrane, I fell to the floor in agony.

In an instant, a colleague rushed over to me and then drove me in her car to the specialist Moorfields Eye Hospital. We sat for a while in a small cubicle waiting for a diagnosis and for analgesic drops to take effect. Around us, we heard other people's moans and groans: children poking each other's eyes and noses with sticks, a man being splashed with bleach by an overzealous cleaner, and other such minor and major catastrophes. One woman was yelling 'what was I thinking?' as they fished a knitting needle out of her socket.

A young man in blue scrubs came, checked me over and announced I had cut my cornea, and that it should heal, but to return if it didn't in the next few days. As he examined me, he seemed perplexed I was really blind in my right eye, and rather than focusing on the newly damaged eye (the left), he asked my favourite question: 'So, are you sure you can't see out of your right eye?' I assured him I could not. He beamed a torch into my blind eye, slightly oblivious to the pain I was in in the other eye. He sighed and said: 'I mean, have you tried cataract surgery? It's really amazing what we can do these days.' I sighed and gave a potted history. 'Yes, I see. You are one of those complicated cases.' I am indeed.

While there is little one can immediately do for a cut cornea other than let it heal on its own, keep it clean with an eye wash and use an analgesic gel, it was a disturbing experience. I shuffled into a taxi and was taken home by the kindly work colleague (now a good friend). At home I lay in my darkened bedroom with an audio book playing quietly in the background and wondered if my life was about to change. My colleague stayed with me for four days, helping me around and bringing me soup. I was deeply grateful.

But as I lay there, I also began to panic. Would I now be permanently and irreversibly blind? Was this the moment when I truly understood sight loss? Away from my intellectual notions of blindness, only did I not want to stop the pain (cutting your cornea is the most invisible pain I have ever felt) but I wanted every inch of my remaining sighted life back and as fast as possible.

I was also angry with my own hypocrisy. Having promoted the joys of blindness for myself and other blind friends, it turned out I was just like the rest of sighted society, who valued sight above all. I did not want to give it up without a fight. A rush of terrifying images ran through my head, and I lived through a few terrible nights of fear and anxiety, possibly more painful than the cut cornea. I was not surprised at my fear: the idea of losing any limb or working part of our bodies – suddenly and overnight – is a primal one. We all wonder how we would cope, continue our lives with jobs, partners and adventures without sight. Will we be treated differently and will people pity us?

While I recovered fully and returned to work, I did ponder far more the question of why I had not pursued a more forceful search for 'fixing myself', as the young man in blue scrubs had thrown at me. And I also became far more aware of the trauma of not seeing coming very suddenly. Not seeing was very real, and I had come close to losing everything all at once. Potentially losing sight overnight is really scary. It is brave to challenge our notions of blindness and reject its past legends, prejudices and myths, but somehow it is also naive – not seeing in a very seeing world is hard and involves a great deal of adaptation. Should I get fixed?

I was also faced with another conundrum that perhaps young Mr Blue Scrubs had not considered. He was promoting cure and fixing – the ultimate medical solution. But this fails to consider that many of us are floating in the middle and canot be fixed.

Mr Scrubs did not bother asking me, for example, if I had considered my options, which I have on many occasions. As my vision has quietly deteriorated, every few years I go and see a variety of specialists to get an update on the latest advances and professional advice. Because I am already totally blind in one eye, any type of operation, doctors say, is 'complicated' and a risky, life-altering event. I am even told that my post-anterior cataract, which has been there since birth (so quite calcified), is right at the back of my eye, near my nerves and capillaries; I am also diabetic and have immune system issues. This might mean that, having not had sight or use of my lens for so many years, my brain may not adapt. Anyone digging around there with a laser, scalpel or even an ultrasound device (think of how glass shatters when subjected to high-pitched sound) might cause irreversible damage, bleeding, infection or permanent blindness.

Indeed, a few cutting-edge experts have offered to do the surgery in a day, and promised that my sight will improve, possibly by up to 50 per cent. But curiously it always comes with a caveat; every specialist I meet will enthuse at their talents, but *all* will add they are not sure – it depends on what they find when they get in there. So most, including my own eye specialist, urge me to leave well alone, and to live my life as I do now. I tend to agree.

Even strangers feel the need to tell me the importance of sharing their family's eyesight stories, and occasionally those of their pets. On one occasion, I ordered a cab, and the lovely cockney driver helped me and my white cane into the back seat. As we waited in a traffic jam, he asked me about my sight. 'Can't you 'ave it fixed then? My mum had hers done last month with a laser.' I quickly responded with my stock answer: 'It's a bit complicated.' He listened, and then dived into a story he had obviously wanted to tell. 'I had a great dog called Bella once,' he said cheerily. 'Real sweetie. Loved her food. Loved her cuddles. Loved kids.' I waited, presuming the story would have a connection to sight.

It did. 'Well, when she got older, she started to bump into things. I took her to the vet, and he said she was an old dog with cataracts, so leave her be. So, I took her home, and she was fine. She smelt out her dinners, she did her business in the garden – not a problem at all.' I uttered some agreement of how happy Bella's life was, particularly in the garden. Then the denouement came. 'She was such a great dog, you know. She let the kids pull her tail, she loved sitting on the sofa with us. But then she went into the coffee table and the DVD player, and cut herself badly. It was sad, but we had to put her down.' He paused thoughtfully, remembering his beloved pooch. I am not sure what courage I was supposed to gain from this story – should I be put down when I can't sniff out my dinners? Or not do my business outside? But to be honest, it was not so offensive. It was just another story in a litany of blind stories I am told *all* the time.

After the cornea-slicing incident, and despite my terror at losing my diminishing sight, the odd thing is that I still find myself asking: in our modern, technology-driven and medically sophisticated world, is it right we always try to fix and cure? Perhaps we don't want to undermine the feeling and safety of knowing there is always a remedial journey if things go wrong. Any deviation from the fixing idea is clearly shocking to the majority of seeing people.

I sense this desire almost every day, as people constantly ask if there is a cure for my sight loss. I am told wondrous stories of how an aunt/cousin/mother/brother had a miraculous operation in the US/Zurich/Cuba. Surely there must be something that can be done for me, everyone asks. But as I have explained above, there is not. It's *complicated*.

The media also reaffirms this omnipresent and possibly indulgent obsession of the miracle eye cure fix. In an edition of *National Geographic* focused on blindness, it read, on the front cover, in giant white letters, 'The End of Blindness', with a subtitle, 'Winning the fight to see'. Behind was a close-up photograph of a human eye, staring out at us. As I flicked through its glossy pages, I found myself overwhelmed at some of the stories (special techniques, implants, technology) and was surprised to see the launch of a competition to rid the world of blindness. The main article was called 'A Cure in Sight', and showed how medical advances and expanding treatments were changing our notions of blindness.

The reporter began his piece, 'Ending blindness may not be a dream'.[2] Inside were a variety of stories about surgery, medical advances, implants and technology that would rid the world of the presumed terrifying state of blindness. I couldn't read half of the articles, mainly because the font was so pale and tiny, but also the pictures of scalpels, of eyes being spliced, and eye diagrams made me feel quite sick, possibly because it was around the time of my cornea crisis.

At the time of writing, there are over 350 articles on the BBC, *New York Times* and London *Times* websites alone on the subject of blindness and cures. The reportage covers everything from stem cell therapy to new glasses that read a chip put in the eye. A recent BBC article reported a treatment of almost futuristic proportions: a young man with a genetic eye condition, having received gene therapy, is now able to see again. 'Just being able to see facial features on my own face is something that I haven't been able to do for years,'[3] he explained to a rather enthusiastic reporter. While in no way would one suggest or

---

[2] Dobbs, David. 'A Cure In Sight', *National Geographic*, September 2016, pp. 35–53.
[3] https://www.bbc.co.uk/news/health-56906002

prevent anyone having lifesaving and life-enhancing surgery, it is also clear why there is a huge incentive and drive to fix and cure any impairment. Academics in the disability field call this view 'ableist', and they are very critical of the medical idea that if you are not whole, integral and perfect, you need to be fixed.

It is fair to say I often used to wonder why sighted people insist on sharing their miracle fixing stories with blind or visually impaired folk, as my blind friends tell me they get the same questions. Partly, I think, it's because people want to prove they are sympathetic to a person's situation – loss of sight is something which we all relate to. We all, at some point, need corrective glasses for reading or seeing further away, and the notion of popping into your local hospital to have a 20-minute cataract operation is now quite mainstream. Even in developing countries, charities zoom in fully equipped high-flying hospitals, and doctors do 200 surgeries a week in far-reaching communities. Of the 285 million people who are estimated to be visually impaired and blind worldwide, the World Health Organization has calculated that 90 per cent are blind because of refractive errors, glaucoma or cataracts,[4] which, if treated, are all fixable.[5]

---

[4] http://www.fightforsight.org.uk/about-the-eye/facts-about-sight-loss/?gclid=CI3y8Y_b48sCFVQ_GwodTqEFVA
[5] https://www.who.int/news-room/fact-sheets/detail/blindness-and-visual-impairment

Attached to this, people can't believe that *something cannot be done*. One psychotherapist even got angry with me because I refused to go and see a specialist he knew in London's famed Harley Street. He implied, with great hostility, that I 'obviously wanted to go blind, otherwise why wouldn't I get another opinion?' This insistence on me being treated and cured has made me very aware about a general need by humanity, even if educated and smart, to fix blindness at all costs. The article from *National Geographic*, the doctor at A&E and the taxi driver all simply confirm this need.

But now I have only 15 per cent sight left and am close to losing all my sight, I have begun to understand that the reason we tell a blind person about fixing stories is because people still sense that losing your sight is the worst fate in the world, as we saw in previous chapters. Sighted people are shocked that someone cannot be fixed. They feel a blind person will be forever in a world of indignity and fear. We endlessly share fixing stories to fill the silence and comfort ourselves.

* * *

Twenty-first-century thinkers and physicians were not the first to be fascinated with fixing of the eye or studying all its components and functions. My classical scholar friends (remember the professor at Cambridge who introduced me to Nandy the Neanderthal?) have, over the years, sent me many articles about ancient practices of healing and curing the eye, including the cutting of the cornea.

Just as Homer was the grandfather of classical literature, so too was Galen of Pergamon (Claudius Galenus, 129–c. 216 AD) the grandfather of anatomy. Galen was one of the first, if not the first, to document how he cut up, investigated and documented the human eye. The eye, he said, was akin to a person wearing many tunics – *tunicae*. Working inwards, he described the eyeball as if describing a person wearing many layers. From Retina (meaning net or mesh in Latin) to Iris (meaning rainbow) and Uvea (a bunch of grapes), the eye was an amazing palimpsest of organs, each having specific tasks that, if out of kilter, would render the entire eye useless.

We know too, from a few fragments of ancient papyrus, that there were continual attempts to cure eye blurring and fog in classical Greco-Roman and Asian empires, usually by the ancient art of couching. This involved placing a narrow metal or bamboo rod in the eye, and the cataract (and lens) being sucked out. There were also cures offered such as squeezing the blood of pigeon's kidneys over a person's eye, or offering sacrifices and votives to gods at various temples. Sadly, we don't know what our ancient anatomists were thinking, but many left us a medical legacy, an encyclopaedic map of the eye, and thus allowing the *possibility* of fixing these optical globes when they went wrong.

While Roman and Greek scholars were obsessed with cutting things up, scholars in Asia and the Middle East were also fascinated with the workings of the eye. Of note was the work and research of the eighth-century philosopher Al-Kindi, the son of the royal house of Kindah, who was labelled 'the philosopher of the Arabs'. He was known for his talents in logic, geometry, mathematics, music, astrology and optics.

Al-Kindi was not overtly an eye fixer or curer, but his investigations into optics did lay the groundwork for Western science and medical practice for centuries to come. His arguments around what made and created a visual ray, and why the eye behaved in the manner it did – including how light bounces off every surface it touches, and how the eye filters this – were astounding discoveries. This knowledge was essential for the creation of spectacles, microscopes and telescopes hundreds of years later. Even the great Renaissance artist Leonardo Da Vinci tried to visualize Al-Kindi's vision of light in his drawings, and referred to him as a genius.

As the centuries rolled on and more work was published about light, sight and its possibilities – in both the East and the West – the eye became increasingly a point of deep scientific enquiry. There was a boom in discoveries and developments which helped shape future operations to cure blindness. In the seventeenth century alone, and standing on the shoulders of Al-Kindi, thinkers such as Willebrord Snellius (often referred to as Snell, according to Dutch archives) and René Descartes formulated the law of the refraction of light. A few years later, Christiaan Huygens discovered light travelled in waves. By the mid-1600s, Sir Isaac Newton proved in grey, rainy Cambridge that light contained a mixture of colours as they refracted in the eye. All of these discoveries, and more, contributed to our understanding of how the eye worked and received light, and its opposite – what stopped light moving into the world and our eyes.

But it was not until the eighteenth century that the real obsession for sight curing took off. While previous eras certainly had men who investigated and explored the nature of light, sight and the eye, almost overnight, it would seem, humankind discovered an ability to surgically operate on the eye – and change a man's destiny. These operations fuelled the ever-expanding public debates around sight and its presumed negative opposite, blindness.

* * *

Suppose a man born blind and now adult and taught by his touch to distinguish between a cube and sphere of the same metal, and rightly of the same bigness, so as to tell, when he felt one and the other, which is the cube, which is the sphere. Suppose the cube and the sphere placed on a table, and the blind made to see; query, whether by his sight, before he touched them, he could now distinguish and tell which is the globe, which the cube?[6]

In one way, researching the eighteenth century was reassuring in thinking about blindness. After centuries of the gods or Jesus being in charge of one's fate, now the world viewed blindness through the eyes of doctors and surgeons. Rather than living above us on lofty Mount Olympus, these change-makers were more likely to be seen in a bloody apron and a blood-stained room with no antiseptics, surrounded by gawping aspiring students. Blindness became a real state of being and one that inquisitive men wanted to explore and investigate.

In an age that has been frequently characterized as 'The Enlightenment' (especially by the German philosopher Immanuel Kant in 1784), this interest was hardly surprising.

---
[6] 'Molyneux's Problem.' https://plato.stanford.edu/entries/molyneux-problem/

The ethos of the era was one where it was one's right and duty to be critical in thought, and to examine the beliefs and premises upon which man created his world – to throw the light of knowledge on old, mythical and archaic notions of the world. To use a dictum once advanced by Horace, Kant challenged his readers to *'Sapore Aude!'* (dare to know), which in turn occupied the minds of key eighteenth-century thinkers such as Jefferson, Voltaire and Diderot. This was an age of reason and curiosity, where the natural world, including man and his body, was systematically analysed, catalogued and debated amongst learned men. Observation became the ethos of the age.

Sight and its theoretic restoration offered some interesting intellectual dilemmas for scholars, especially for the English philosopher John Locke (1632–1704). Locke, a non-practising medical doctor, considered many topics, but he was particularly interested in how man gleaned knowledge, and whether information was obtained through his physical senses, rather than an innate or God-given sense of internal ideas and rules. Man was able to know for himself, Locke argued, what his world was through his ears, sense of touch, taste, smell and, above all, sight. Locke asked: if we did not have one of our key senses out of the five, such as sight, how could we understand and experience the world?

These questions, published in a series of essays entitled *An Essay on Human Understanding* (1688), became even more complex when an Irish academic, William Molyneux, wrote to Locke asking if a man born blind would know the difference between a globe and a sphere if he had not seen such objects before. Five years later, Locke declared Molyneux had provided an 'ingenious problem' to which he had thought long and hard over an answer: 'I am of the opinion that ... the blind man, at first sight, would *not* be able with certainty to say which was the globe, which the cube.' This was because, Locke argued, a newly sighted person would have to learn what the globe or sphere would be. Interestingly, Molyneux did not mention that his own wife had become blind in the first year of their marriage. Nor did Locke, as far as we know, ask any blind man or woman what they thought or had experienced. But the debate became mainstream to the point that the constant repetition of the words 'blind' and 'sight' in the educated arenas of pamphlets and royal reports further pushed blindness as an idea and a subject to be discussed in the mainstream salons, clubs and coffee houses of the reading elite. Blindness was no longer hidden, or mystical, but part of life.

While there was no agreement over what a blind man could or could not see after a *theoretical* restoration of sight (and no one seemed to stop and think what a blind man thought about these questions), within the space of five years, the debate inspired philosophers from France, Italy and Germany to respond to the question. Seventeen years after Locke's essay was published, Bishop George Berkeley, over in Ireland, joined the debate, writing that he was fascinated by the difference between the senses of sight and touch, and asked 'whether there be any idea common to both senses'.

* * *

When he first saw ... he knew not the shape of any Thing, nor any one Thing from another ... but upon being told what things were, whose form he before knew from feeling, he would carefully observe, that he might know them again; but having too many Objects to learn at once, he forgot many of them.[7]

Given this backdrop of debate and scientific discovery (and interest in blindness), it was hardly surprising that the most famous and significant change to man's view of

---

[7] Cheselden, William. 'An account of some observations made by a young gentleman, who was born blind, or lost his sight so early, that he had no remembrance of ever having seen, and was couch'd between 13 and 14 years of age.' *Philosophical Transactions*, 35 (1727–28): 447–50.

blindness in the mid-eighteenth century was by a young doctor called William Cheselden, who was keen to make his name in the court and medical academy. While there were many reports of eye cures and miracles in France (Jacques Daviel, the oculist extraordinaire to Louis XV) and England (John Freke), Cheselden's report of 1728 regarding his cataract operation took the medical fraternity, academia and public by storm.

Born in 1688, Cheselden was known at first as a physician of great speed in excising kidney and gallstones, with astonishing survival rates. In 1728, after years of climbing the greasy career pole of medical notoriety, he wrote in a report[8] to the Royal Society that he had conquered one of man's greatest impairments: blindness. Cheselden wrote that he had successfully treated a patient, who was 'a youth of thirteen or fourteen ... born blind ... And suffered from Cataracts ... which seem to hang as if glass in broken jelly'.

In many ways, Cheselden's report was just another case study by an aspiring medical professional, keen to have his work known and acknowledged by his peers and contemporaries. The vocabulary was clinical, the patient was anonymous, and there was absolutely no acknowledgement of the patient's experience – which must

---

[8]Cheselden, 'An account ... '.

have been painful, given the lack of analgesic. Indeed, he argued the operation was successful because he asked the patient what he could see, and the patient replied he could see something – colour and shapes – and more than the blurry mess so many other attempts had produced. Cheselden's 'blind youth' provided objective data and empirical facts that could help understand blindness and answer the deep questions Locke and Molyneux had started debating thirty years before.

Yet when the patient was asked the 'Molyneux question' – i.e. whether a blind man with sight anew could tell the difference between a globe and cube (and, in this case, the difference between a dog and a cat) – he could not answer. Cheselden tells us that the young man could not tell the difference between anything, unless he used touch rather than his newfound sight. Cheselden's operation was simply a means to an end; it offered an answer to the philosophical question Locke and Molyneux had posited, and demonstrated that a person needed experience and time to learn to see.

Cheselden was not the only surgeon to ride on the back of Enlightenment obsessions with fixing and curing. Many self-professed physicians and oculists attempted to cure blindness, and thus gain notoriety and large fees. Many families, rich or poor, turned to itinerant self-declared eye specialists, who promised to fix blind people with ointments, magnetic treatments and painful procedures. As many were to discover too, often such attempts made the condition much worse than the original ailment or impairment. Many lost their sight from these interventions, including the famous composer Johann Sebastian Bach, who was said to have died after complications from eye surgery.

Even when it was clear that a 'cure' for blindness was ludicrous or redundant, the push to at least attempt a cure was seen as the only way forward. There was a sense that not attempting was a failure of an individual's duty to themselves and society.

Many were treated by quacks and charlatans who claimed to treat every disease of the eye. Supposed cures included having one's head immersed in salt or vinegar water to remove the presumed obstructions of the sight line. Doctors in Vienna in 1730 reported placing leeches on the eye, electric currents on eyeballs, and encasing heads in plaster for months on end to force blockages out of the eye. In England, surgeon John Chevalier was so confident of his own procedure that he attended to the composer Handel, but only caused his condition to worsen. In Germany, similar self-promoters offered their services. On a flyer published in 1746, for example, the Prussian oculist Joseph

Hilmer, who claimed erroneously to have performed the first cataract operations, had flyers printed which proclaimed: 'Good people are invited to witness him give sight to the blind using his secret eye potion that works in minutes.'[9] The poor, the doctor added, could be treated 'free of charge' by coming along at the stated time. He also offered surgery, but there was little for flinching or fearfulness: 'He operated with such impertinent audacity and was so rough that when one woman shrieked in pain, he gave her a clip around the ear, when he already had his needle in her eye.'[10]

Understandably, few reported that most interventions did not work, and many people died from infection and haemorrhaging. There is also no evidence as to what blind people themselves thought about these treatments and the parade of cures in the booming publicity around such miraculous moments – though one can imagine that, without analgesics, it was immensely painful and frightening.

Despite such public failures, the media of the day pushed forward a miracle cure narrative. Pamphlets, journals, newspapers and a vast array of essays offered a stage where

---

[9]Tunstall, Kate E. *Blindness and Enlightenment: An Essay, with a New Translation of Diderot's* Essay on the Blind, *1749* (Continuum, 2011), p. 128.
[10]Tunstall, *Blindness and Enlightenment*, p. 129.

a cast of blind characters who had no choice or say in the matter were allegedly cured, then paraded, gawped at and celebrated – a phenomenon that continued well into the nineteenth century and beyond. In July 1709 *Tatler* reported the story of William Jones of Surrey's treatment by the oculist Roger Grant. The operation was reported in reverential terms: 'When the Patient first received the Dawn of Light, there appeare'd such an Ecstasy in his Action that he seemed ready to swoon away in the Surprise of Joy and Wonder . . .' Similar stories appeared in the aptly named *Spectator* and *Observer* magazines.

Above all, just as medieval farces distanced sighted from blind people in the public arena, so too did the reporting of operations and miracles. While such entertainment was certainly not as bad as medieval games, the reporting of Cheselden's extraordinary accomplishments hid the fact that such treatments were not available to most blind people, and even if the patient could find a specialist, they would more than likely be subject to pain and suffering.

* * *

With such a hive of miracle cures and fixing operations, it was helpful to find that, running parallel to miracle sight-restoration stories and super-duper cures, there are hundreds of tales about blind people who were offered the lure of a cure and either regretted it or rejected it. While doctors and surgeons wanted to enhance their noble reputations as life changers and life savers, it seemed that not everyone succumbed to being fixed.

The first 'fixing doesn't always work' stories I read were about those people who, after restoring their sight with surgery, change temperament. The extraordinary ophthalmologist and gay rights activist Patrick Trevor-Roper (brother of famous historian Hugh Trevor-Roper) wrote movingly, in *The World Through Blunted Sight* (1970), of how blindness and its restoration affected his patients in different ways. Some shifted from being shy and quiet to being gregarious and confident, which he attributed to their using their voices to find their way – like echo location. Others became the complete opposite, terrified to make fools of themselves after years of confident existence. He wrote too about how the slow loss of sight could affect writers, artists and musicians, which, in his view, could often be to their advantage, as their loss of sight forced them to focus on aspects of their work that they had not considered before. As was the norm with the medical world, he did not offer space for blind people to comment themselves on his views, but at least he thought about it.

There are similar stories told by Dr Oliver Sacks, the writer and neurologist, who himself had sight loss from eye cancer. Aside from penning his best-selling books, *The Man Who Mistook His Wife for A Hat* and *Awakenings*, Sacks also wrote a beautiful essay in the *New Yorker* in 1993[11] about the impact of a sight-restoring operation on a blind patient called Virgil. Virgil, a 45-year-old Oklahoman, was referred to Sacks because he had an operation that restored his vision. But instead of what his wife imagined would be happiness and joy in the sighted world, Virgil became depressed, despondent and withdrawn. He missed the touch world he had inhabited for so long. He felt lost and frightened in the visual world in which he had woken up.

Despite Virgil never having had a visual memory, having relied on touch to function, he found his nights full of nightmares while his brain tried to make sense of the visual world it was now experiencing. As Virgil withdrew, he lost his job, his home, and his will to participate in life. Virgil and Dr Sacks met a few times and spoke on the phone, and Sacks wrote about how he tried to understand how bewildered Virgil was when he woke up after his operation, but even more so as he began to function in the world.

What is shocking about these stories is how the sighted world did not, and still does not, understand why newly sighted people don't find that having sight is so marvellous,

---

[11] Sacks, Oliver. 'To See and Not See'. *The New Yorker* (May 1993).

glorious and essential to human existence. Some 'cured' people's depression and withdrawal from the world come as much from themselves as from the pressure of the expectations of the sighted world around them. Virgil's previously blind brain did not understand how to process any of the visual world because it had not learnt it. Sacks believed Virgil was suffering 'acute visual fatigue'. I will not relate the entire tale here but do urge you to read it online – it is so worth reading in full.

Sacks was not the only writer to document how operations to cure sight loss were not always successful.[12] Marius Von Senden, who reviewed over three hundred years' worth of eye surgery data in a book called *Space and Sight* (1932), concluded that not every patient wanted eye surgery or, having had it, had enough motivation through the change from one world to another. He tells of one patient who felt so threatened by sight (which meant he would leave his haven of a blind asylum) that he threatened to pierce and then pull his eyes out. Many patients also reverted to 'behaving blind' or 'refusing to see' after an operation. Sociologists and medical specialists have reported similar stories.

---

[12]See notes by Alberto Valvo, *Sight Restoration after Long Term Blindness* (American Foundation for the Blind, 1971).

It's worth reiterating that none of these doctors were saying that anyone with an eye condition shouldn't have an eye operation. I certainly know from having my small incident cutting my cornea: when you are suffering or in pain, get help. Medicine and surgery are phenomenal in so many ways; it would take more than a few volumes to explain how far and how much we have achieved in the past thousand years to alleviate human distress.

However, I think what chimed with me was how Sacks understood how restoring vision might not be the only option for someone who was blind or even losing their sight, and it might not make their lives more valuable or liveable. Sometimes living with what you have is good enough. Key to thinking about fixing blindness, therefore – for me at least – is less about whether we should or should not be fixed, but more, how do we live with ambiguity and complexity if we do not wish to be 'restored'? What if being blind or visually impaired is simply just a different way of being on this planet? It might not be easy, but perhaps no life is.

As I read these 'non-fix' and non-miracle stories, I began to understand that while surgery and other such fixes were and are miraculous and a good thing, what underlines these discussions is the question of whether my life, or any other blind person's life, is less valuable than a fully sighted life. As my consultant said to me, 'you are so used to the life you have, it's not clear how much you would gain, even if your eyesight was improved'. Is having an operation something that would make my life easier?

It might. But there again, it might not.

* * *

While my sashay into the eighteenth century was at times painful, I did find some relief in the idea that blindness was beginning to be de-sacralized, albeit by the sighted community. Many pushed and continued to objectify the idea that all blindness was a burden and a misfortune (and thus must be fixed), and it became very much part of man's great quest to know and literally see the world. Surgery proved how blindness could be transformed by the application of science into therapy, and how the responsibility of the blind person to be cured shifted from the gods to the individual. Blind people were perceived as 'victims' of their condition rather than mere guilty sinners and objects that proved man's ability to overcome impairments. But a few people rebelled against such thinking and affected me deeply – one of whom was the little-known blind musician Maria Theresia von Paradis.

To many, the story of Maria Theresia von Paradis was one of musical talent and conquest over the courts and salons of Europe. Born in 1759 to the Court Councillor of Empress Maria Theresa of Austria, Theresia went blind aged two after a bout of a serious unknown illness. While her family were devastated, they were comforted that she showed musical talent from an early age. The empress was so deeply impressed with the young girl's playing of the piano that she granted a royal pension to fund her musical training.

By 1773, Theresia was so well-admired that, it is said, Mozart composed a piano concerto for her, and Antonio Salieri, the court composer, dedicated an organ concerto to her. By 1784, Joseph Haydn had also joined the fan club. She wrote over thirty sonatas and at least five operas (many are lost). She died in 1824, in her sixties, having established one of the leading schools for blind musicians in Europe, according to the press of the day.

Hidden behind her musical fame, however, was a daily life of extreme pain and endless medical treatment. As with other blind women of her class and education, she was subjected to an extraordinary variety of treatments to cure her blindness. Every possibility was explored, including electrolysis on her eyeballs, her head encased in plaster for three months, and years of purgatives and diuretics. The doctor who was to later treat her and claim to cure her, Franz Anton Mesmer, described the treatment she had been subjected to: 'For over two months her head was covered by an ointment producing continual suppuration. For a number of years purgatives and diuretics were used, including pulsatilla and valerian root.'[13] For all her talent, Theresia suffered physically throughout her life.

Moreover, her personal and public life came under massive scrutiny, whether on her tours or when undertaking new medical treatments. According to the *Paris Journal* of November 1776, she attempted a new and unconventional treatment. Theresia's father, Baron von Paradis, contacted the eccentric, but none-the-less famous, Franz Anton Mesmer in a bid to see if he could cure her. Dr Mesmer was renowned in Vienna for his unconventional medical practices, which argued man should cultivate a relationship to the body through 'animal magnetism'. He described this magnetism as the body's dynamic ebb and flow of energy. Such magnetism could be reached through hypnosis and the use of magnets, and then pressing upon the hypochondrium (the point just below the diaphragm), remaining in this position for hours. After a while, he would stand up and walk over to a glass harmonium, where he

---

[13] Mesmer, Franz Anton. *Mesmerism – A translation of the original medical and scientific writings of F. A. Mesmer.* Complied and translated by George J. Block (William Kaufman, 1980).

would play eerie and mystical music. Many patients reported convulsions and then being cured after such treatments.

Mesmer first met Theresia in March 1776. He wrote in his notes the family had employed 'every method most suitable for this infirmity' and that Theresia was 'out of her mind after having been subjected to so much pain'. After taking Theresia under his care in his own home, and after only three weeks submitting to his ministrations, he revealed to her father that, having treated her blindness with hypnosis, the harmonium and magnets, he had cured her. He wrote that both her eyes had readjusted to their natural organic state and her sight had returned. He even reported that, as she became familiar with his dimly lit study, upon seeing his nose she laughed at the ugliness of its proportions.

At first, his 'cure' of Vienna's most talented daughter was celebrated by the court. Her family were thrilled and praised Dr Mesmer publicly. Many applied to meet the young musician to see for themselves. Yet there was one worrying consequence of the cure. While Theresia allegedly could see the piano from which she had carved out her career, she seemed to have lost her confidence, staring at the keyboard as if she did not recognize it. She had lost her talent – the one 'compensation' for losing her sight. It was perhaps not surprising, therefore, that three months after the alleged miracle, her father declared to the court that she was still blind and had, in fact, never regained her sight. He argued that they had been mistaken and misled by Mesmer. It is not clear what motivated this dramatic about-turn. But it is likely he knew that if Theresia could not play the piano, the comfortable royal pension that supported her, and her career, might disappear.

After a lengthy investigation, where harsh epistles were published – literally at dawn – between Baron von Paradis and Mesmer, the Austrian medical establishment agreed to investigate. They found no evidence his methods worked, and asked Mesmer to stop practising or leave Vienna. Unable to defend his name, he fled, and after a few years wandering around Europe retreated to Paris, where his methods also came under scrutiny. Here the doctor submitted to a scientific committee from the Royal Academy of Sciences in France, who also declared him a fake. He died in Lausanne, Switzerland, where it was said half the country believed in his cures and the other half thought him a quack.

While it is almost impossible to know if Theresia really did regain her sight, it is interesting, if not sad, to realize so much of the information we have about her concerns her medical treatment. We know from press cuttings that after the Mesmer debacle, she returned to a successful career playing the fortepiano and composing. She went on tour around Europe, including France and Britain, and met and influenced the founder of one of the most important blind schools in Paris, Valentin Haüy. He helped her establish one of the first-ever musical schools for blind musicians in Vienna. We also know from catalogues in 1824 that she had written five operas, nineteen instrumental works and several cantatas, some of which are still played today. And unlike Mozart, Haydn and a few other known women composers, who died penniless or unpublished, she had what few musicians had in the era – a successful profession and an income.

* * *

Theresia's life and work has often carried me while researching and writing this book, and, if truth be told, distracted me. Wishing to give her a voice, a group of fellow disabled women got together with myself, the brilliant modern composer Errollyn Wallen and co-librettist Nicola Werenowska. Together, we co-created a modern opera about Theresia's life called *The Paradis Files*, imagining what she would have felt, the treatments she had, the love we imagined she had for Mozart, and the difficult relationship she must have had with her parents, given they were reliant on her musical pension to sustain themselves.

Amazingly, from the kernels of a chat over lunch, the opera was picked up, funded, went on tour around the UK and had a premiere at London's Southbank Centre. The UK and opera press could not believe they had not heard of this vibrant, clever and talented woman, who was blind. I smiled quietly inside when I read the reviews, because not only did Theresia show me how often blind women are not given the credit they deserve – particularly in a patriarchal court system – but she also showed that just by living her life she had a choice as to her career and treatment. In short, she carved out a life for herself.

It is true that, unlike most women of her era, she had wealth, contacts and talent. It seems the combination allowed her great freedom and the liberty to use her skills. Some people ask: if she had not been blind, would she have had so much attention?

What I reply is that we know Theresia had a prominent place in the musical court, and she was deeply respected by her musical peers – not an easy task in a male-dominated world. We know she created a music school for blind children and passed her learnings and inventions on to the next generation. Blindness might have been part of her 'unique selling point' and probably attracted much attention – the London *Times* called her 'The Blind Enchantress', after all – but I love that none of these labels prevented her from pursuing her musical career or having a colourful love life (we think). And while we don't have any first-person commentary from her, we know from other composers' views of her (especially Mozart and his sister Nannerl) that she chose a life away from curing and fixing. Her blindness was *not* her focus – playing and teaching music was. Blind or not, she might not have been published anyway, simply because she was a woman, limited to the courts and salons of the day, rather than the great public opera houses.

I admire Theresia because she lived beyond the endless curing and fixing ethic of her time, and actively understood her own success was not dependent on having or regaining sight. While she did not write about herself, we have a sense of her choices by the tours, the compositions and her Viennese school.

Perhaps this is the very lesson we all need to learn: with enough support, education, finance and belief in ourselves, we can choose. We don't have to bow to medical or society's pressures, bunkum or quackery. We don't have to bow to the court – whether eighteenth-century or twenty-first.

Ever.

5

Learning it

Education, education, education

My sister, whom I adore, lives in Iowa, USA.

Each year we try and have an adventure just the two of us. Either we try a new place, experience or skill, and over the years, we have had many travels together – Amsterdam, Rome, New York – where she relied on me for cultural context and I relied on her quirky, if not eccentric, ability to describe the world around me. One year, opting to stay close to home, we decided to take a drive out to a town called Vinton where we had found that the 'Iowa Blind and Sight Saving School' was still running.

We had decided to go not only because I was writing my 'bloody history book' (to quote the sibling), but also because we discovered, via a wonderful friend and scholar, Dr Brian

Miller,[1] that Mary Ingalls, the sister of the writer of the *Little House on the Prairie* children's books, had been a student and teacher at the school. Somewhat overlooked in the books and the 1970s TV series (it was *always* about Laura's adventures), Mary Ingalls became blind aged 14 and, according to the TV series, became a teacher for other blind kids. Allegedly, she married a fellow blind teacher, Adam Kendall. Sadly, the *Prairie* stories did not document her life or her views on blindness, so we thought it might be good to explore where blind women of the mid-nineteenth century found an education.

Driving through miles and miles of cornfields which bristled golden and wide across the prairies, we pulled off the interstate and followed the only road into (and out of) Vinton. My sister described, as she was prone to do with her visually impaired sister, a dusty abandoned town; shuttered shops and grey-looking people staring at the new visitors. We drove past what seemed to be the only open retail outlets – the post office, the diner and the general store – and then back onto the road. There, on the horizon, out of the smooth sea of gold, stood an enormous cream

---

[1] Miller, Brian R. 'Speaking for themselves: The blind civil rights movement and the battle for the Iowa Braille School.' *Iowa Research Online* (2013).

edifice. My sister said brightly it reminded her of the plantation houses in *Gone with the Wind*, but after the Civil War – faded, forlorn and neglected. It stood in the middle of a field with neoclassical columns, a dome, and north and south wings with verandas radiating out each side. Gravel paths around the sides leading to gardens. We almost expected ladies with full hooped dresses to sweep out on to the verandas.

Entering a wide marble front hall covered by the dome, we found ourselves at an old wooden reception desk, where a kindly middle-aged woman smelling of rose water was thrilled to have visitors. 'You from England?' she swelled, and immediately yelled for her colleague Cathleen to show us around. As we waited, my sister explained the space: two elegant wide staircases leading up each side behind the desk, which later we were to learn were different stairs for boys and girls and led to their dormitories. Rails along the corridors guided students, as well as Braille signs on all the doors. 'You blind?' our hostess asked. I nodded and brought forth my cane. 'Great!' she cooed, as if I had answered a question correctly, and off we went on the tour.

Thrilled to share the story of great goodness and charity, our guide told us the school had been founded by a local philanthropist, Mr Vinton, in 1852 to provide education and skills for 'the blind' across the US Midwest. It was considered one of the leading training centres of its era, and families considered themselves lucky if they could get their blind children a place. Sent from age six from around the Midwest, pupils were given lessons in reading Braille, mathematics, music, geography and writing. Attending Vinton also meant learning and becoming self-sufficient; it was mandatory to attend classes on specialist skills and development training, not to mention key domestic and mobility skills that would prepare them for employment in the outside world. These included sewing, beadwork, broom and brush making, hammock and fly net tying. Some pupils reported spending six months just learning to thread a needle.

As we shuffled around, I felt the school smelt not only of disinfectant, but paternalism of the worst kind. It was in the middle of nowhere, and it being spring break there were no kids playing, yelling, or laughing. But what depressed me the most, however, was that 'the blind' were separated from the general population. The students could not leave easily, and in fact often stayed for a decade or more, without returning home. Furthermore, boys and girls were kept apart, even sitting in different sections of the classroom for lessons.

There were strict rules for everything: rules to get up, rules on how to dress, rules on how to eat and rules on what kids could read and learn and when. Even rules on how to wash and groom oneself. My heart sank as we trundled around the classrooms and workshops and dormitories with their high ceilings, wooden desks and clearly demarked lanes of sitting, walking and engaging in conversation. Rules on how to be blind.

Finally, we were taken to the exhibition space back in the main hallway, which showed visitors the past glories of the school. Here we learnt about Mary Ingalls, who had attended the school in 1881.

Unfortunately, unlike the sentimental TV series, the real Mary never became a teacher, nor ever married, but returned to South Dakota and spent her time making hammocks and fly nets to support the family's income. In fact, there were no voices of blind men or women in the exhibition at all, just the photographs of children leaning over desks learning Braille and basket weaving. We did not learn much about how Mary experienced the school (she was there for seven years), or whether she even wanted to attend it, but we did hear she had good grades, despite missing a year of school when she was ill. She could even, it was reported, quote Robert Burns in a Scottish accent by heart, which seemed to impress our guide.

Our guide was also enthusiastic about the changes the school had undergone as it moved into the twentieth century. The good news was that not only did it continue as a school, she said, but it opened its doors to blind adults who needed skill training. She described black and white photos from the 1950s showing 'happy' blind people making baskets, brushes and woodwork. My sister, holding my hand tightly, anticipating my reaction, read to me the words from the large 1960s poster which was prominently displayed above the exhibition. In huge font and below in Braille, the words read: 'BLIND PEOPLE CAN WORK, AND THEY DO!' Men and women were pictured facing the camera grinning, holding various tools of their trade: finished brushes and brooms. It made us cough nervously; we politely thanked our hostess and left.

* * *

We drove back in silence, but when we got home and sat in the blissfully unruly chaos that was my sister's living room (a house with few rules), she said: 'I mean, it could have been you shut away in that dreadful place. It could have been you.' I nodded and sighed, mostly in gratitude that it was not.

While we both completely understood that each era has its own notions of what is best for its citizens, the idea that my only choice would have been to be sent away simply to learn to read, sew, sing or make brooms was scary. We hated the slogan of blind people being able to work – 'and they do!' (now a well-worn motto in our house) – and felt relieved that our own childhood, despite all its vicissitudes, gave us both tremendous choices, albeit in different ways.

In fact, we decided, my parents' view on disability had been quite unusual in its time. It seemed in direct opposition to Vinton school's ethos. Not only was I part of the family, but I was obliged to participate in absolutely everything that other nice, privileged middle-class girls did. Above all, my sister regaled me with how independent my parents insisted I be. Aged thirteen months, I would sit in the middle of the floor of the kitchen, peach-like in my frilly pink knickers, wearing my enormous Perspex-rimmed glasses, and issue directives. I ordered my then toddler sister to fetch and carry whatever I fancied.

It was quite a ruse: yell for something (dolly/teddy) and suddenly it would come to you. But when my mother witnessed such behaviour, she was furious. 'You are not to fetch and carry for your sister,' she said, talking to my sister as if catching one of the dogs sniffing in the dishwasher. 'Why not?' asked the headstrong older sibling, not used to having her service interrupted. 'She may not see very well, but she has to learn to find things for herself.' Sadly for my sister this was the end of playing 'air-hostess', but I still boss her around today to make up for it.

There were a few other clues, however, that perhaps my parents' Dunkirk spirit was problematic. As I entered the world of schools and young life, we immediately encountered many other people's ignorance and prejudice about vision impairments – primary school being the first obstacle. Some teachers, for example, felt it was not certain that I would be able to attend mainstream school at all. When I was about four, after a term at my new primary school, my mother noticed I had stopped reading. The school, a small local one, was considered academically sound and catered to parents who wanted their children to be polite, well-mannered and ready for middle/upper class living. We wore navy blue dresses piped in white stitching, and stuck straw boaters on our heads in summer. In winter we wore navy blue capes and hats with red pom-poms on the top. My sister had attended two years before and had been very happy. All went well and as I joined, my parents sat down with the teachers and carefully explained about my eyesight. As per their style, they insisted that they wanted no special treatment for their child. 'Treat her as everyone else. She gets along superbly,' my mother instructed. 'Just point her in the right direction if she gets lost.' The straw hat and navy dress were acquired, and off I went.

A few weeks later, however, I was sent home with a letter for my parents. Mrs D, the headteacher, wrote that while obviously 'Selina is a sweet-natured child', she thought I might have learning difficulties, which she was unable to support. Apparently, I sat in the back of the class throwing my ABC blocks about and yelling. They had in fact placed me at the back of the class (instead of the front where I might have seen what was going on), and my mother, a fiercely loyal soul, stormed into Mrs D's office demanding an explanation.

I am not sure what happened in that office – my mother says there were some blows with handbags – but given her strong Celtic determination I can imagine the row. Letters were sent between home and school, and suggestions made that I have my mental agility tested. Off we went to some clinic where not only did they find I was just bored at my primary, but that I was allegedly two steps away from joining MENSA. The boater and navy outfit were ditched, and the next week I started at another school where books were plentiful, I wore my own clothes, and I sat in the front row. I thrived and stayed until I was ten.

Over the years, there were other battles with teachers that my parents fought on my behalf – some minor, some major – but the philosophy of 'normality' persisted. By the time I was twelve, my parents decided to send me to a small girl's boarding school about an hour and a half from home. While not very academic, it was calm and pleasant, and not very demanding. I was very often left to my own devices and told 'not to worry' if I could not participate. Part of this was because the staff at the school had a very limited notion of what visually impaired kids could achieve, and if I was lazy it was because I was excused so many things – art classes, sports, almost anything that involved vision. In turn, and in retrospect, I think I even excused myself from trying to do things which many blind people today take for granted, such as swimming or running – though my parents insisted on the former.

While I did sit in the front of the class, even this did not help me see the blackboard, and I spent many lessons drifting off in my own little dreams, writing short stories in my head, as I could not see the board. One teacher said to me as I went into an A-level exam: 'Don't worry. We don't expect you to pass, do just the best you can.' It's not surprising I left school with very bad grades, which I had opportunities to amend later – oh, and attend prestigious universities.

Away from school, my parents also decided I should be given all the opportunities my fully sighted sister had. This included learning to ski (well), play tennis (badly – never saw a ball ever), ride and cook. I spent many happy holidays with my family, and it gave my sister and I many shared experiences and memories. I particularly loved sitting behind my father on his motorbike and feeling the sway of the bike as we turned corners, my hair flapping beneath the helmet.

Weirdly, after a few years of refusal, I even learnt to ski with my father hovering just in front of me, yelling 'turn, hup, turn, hup' as we went down the mountain. Such adventures gave me a freedom that many do not expect me to have. As my father taught me, so much of skiing is based on the relationship of your body to the mountain, and not on seeing – even one movement of your toe in your boot can alter your ski direction. Obviously, I have learnt to emergency stop when anyone yells 'rock!' or even 'cliff!' and I have used my skiing lessons as I have learnt to walk with a white cane.

My parents – rather unexpectedly – had a few unusual ideas about their visually impaired daughter. This included teaching me to drive a car, even though the law said I did not have enough sight. When close friends gingerly asked what on earth I was doing behind a wheel, my father answered briskly: 'Well, you never know! One day she might be in a car and her driver has a heart attack. She needs to know how to get the car to safety.' The good news is that I learnt to drive on my grandmother's farm (not on a public road) and many sheep spent many hours running far and wide from my attempts. At the very worst, I did drive quite a few times into the gate, the ditch and, well, the hen house. But the very best memory is that I can still feel my father's tall frame shaking with laughter as we sat upside-down in the toppled Land Rover. 'Don't worry, darling,' he spluttered, 'but please do stop when I tell you to stop!' In retrospect, I do wonder when they thought I would use my driving skills.

As we sat and chatted at my sister's home in Iowa, we decided that my parents' insistence I should have as integrated a life with the world as possible was incredibly helpful. We both felt my lack of sight did not define me, nor prevent me from leading an active, rather fun childhood. It also gave my sister a very clear idea of disability and the education to know that whatever your impairment, you are part of society, not separate from it. This is a philosophy with which she has brought up her own children.

But we also suspected my parents resisted the 'blind people can work, and they do!' attitude to blindness because they were a little bit in denial too. They did not like to think their child would be treated any differently from the rest of the planet and understood the damage and isolation it could inflict. Even in the rebellious punk-rocking 1970s era into which I was born, the stigma around blindness was (and still is) pervasive.

I think my parents were trying to protect me not so much from what they thought of me and my needs – a cherished and perky daughter – but the assumptions made by others about how the world would accept me.

It turns out our hunch was right. In my late twenties, my mother did once bring up the subject of educating disabled kids. After hearing a debate in Parliament about the subject – specifically, whether more disabled kids should be brought into mainstream education – she said thoughtfully: 'You know, we sent you to all the mainstream schools because we wanted you to have the most "normal" life we could give you. We already thought you were under so much pressure going to see so many doctors and eye specialists, so we thought sending you to a special school would make you feel even more isolated. We thought if you could cope with being part of the mainstream, you should stay in it. It might not have been the best solution, but it was the best one we knew at the time.'

My sister and I have often discussed the dilemmas of being a parent, as she has two strapping lads, and we always come back to two things. First, despite our parents' protestations I could do anything (which, of course, one can't), it also had the unwanted side effect of me being in denial about my impending sight loss. It has taken me a long time, for example, to accept that I do have limits (sighted or not) and that I should and can ask for help without negating my own value. Asking someone to help you across the road is not asking someone to run your life or make your decisions for you. It is simply crossing the road. Indeed, asking people *not* to help you cross the road, because they are too keen to help, is also very important. I have also stumbled around and pretended I could cope for far longer than I needed to, and I have often felt immensely lonely in my ability to manage my lack of sight. So perhaps super optimism and courage must have a balance: there are limits, and sometimes you really can't drive, sighted or not.

But secondly, my sister and I both agree that our parents' philosophy also gave us both immense confidence in ourselves as women and supported us in going to radically thinking universities. Our parents' mantra was we must think for ourselves. We have always had a sense that we could aim high (if we wanted to) and follow whatever we wanted to do, whether it be a teacher and a mother in Iowa, or a journalist in London, married to an 'eccentric Oxford don'. Unlike so many other visually impaired/blind women, I was given an opportunity to have a voice and my own agency – a chance Mary Ingalls did not. We still do not know how she experienced the world and what she might have done, had she had the chance. It would have been nice to know what she really thought.

Above all, we decided, it is a difficult dilemma facing every parent; whether being sent away to learn or home schooled, blind or not, each child needs different things, depending on their character and needs. Hardly surprising, therefore, to find such dilemmas were constantly debated in the nineteenth century by well-educated, wealthy and clever white men, some of whom were blind.

What I did not expect, until I started digging a bit deeper, was that some of these calls for change and self-determination came from well-educated, wealthy, outspoken and blind *women*.

* * *

The ethics and educational morals of the nineteenth century have filled up many a history volume over the years, and I would not dare to cover all its horrors and successes in one chapter.

A brief background, however, never goes amiss, and it's interesting to learn that the ethos of the nineteenth century was very much one of morality, self-sufficiency and charity. After the bloody crucible and unrest of the French Revolution, there was a great push across Europe by the new ruling elite to appear (at least) as leaders of a caring society. This meant they must help the most disadvantaged, including the 'so called' poor, the destitute and impaired, which included the blind population. No longer governed by king, nobility or the Church, the question of how to run a country, including its impoverished, destitute and 'defected' people, became deeply pertinent.

The wealthy and aristocratic returned to a spirit of self-sacrifice and philanthropic projects, particularly towards the less fortunate. They now regularly used words such as 'infirm' and 'defected'.

The modus operandi for such philanthropic projects varied in each country, but mostly revolved around the creation of schools, institutions and charities. While charity began at home, education and employment also gave rise to the notion of self-sufficiency, and this was an ethos that permeated across the West throughout the century. The requirements for eligibility varied. Some insisted on blind candidates being Christian or belonging to a particular type of church. Some provided for age groups, or children.

Others, like the Royal Blind Pension Society of the United Kingdom, granted pensions 'without regard to sect or creed' provided candidates were of 'good moral character'. Who decided what 'moral character' meant was usually dictated by self-appointed directors of the local charity. Some criteria were so strict that most applicants were excluded. Disparate though their ethos often was, they were all engaged in the common thread of social improvement.[2]

The first kernels of educating blind people in the Western hemisphere – or perhaps the word 'schooling' would be better – came from France. A few institutions for 'the blind' had been operating since the early Middle Ages across Europe, including the caves of Cappadocia, where monks created a 'singing school' for blind warriors. Such establishments had usually been set up for war-wounded blind people in bygone years and could only help a very limited number of blind people. Many places were heavily religious, regulated, and offered a strictly institutional way of living. Daily life was extremely ordered, and each differed as to whom and how many they would allow in.

The late eighteenth and early nineteenth centuries still saw blindness as a deficit. Such an idea was particularly

---

[2]Phillips, Gordon. *The Blind in British Society: Charity, State and Community 1780 to 1900* (Ashgate, 2004), p. 11.

well argued by the blind poet Dr Thomas Blacklock, who was commissioned to define blindness in 1775 for the early editions of the *Encyclopaedia Britannica*. Reverberating with the language and vocabulary of the era, blindness was still defined as a negative. A blind person is 'deprived' of the use of his eyes. The blind man is denied the 'glorious variety of the visible creation'. The vocabulary still rendered blindness as a great tragedy ('inexpressible misfortune') and one that needed compensating. But Blacklock also advocated the need for blind people to have access to education and cultural knowledge:

> *By what means is this inexpressible misfortune [blindness] to be compensated or alleviated to those who sustain it? What advantages and consolations they may derive from it; of what acquisitions may they be susceptible; what are the proper means of their improvement; or by what culture may they become useful to themselves and important members of society?*[3]

Unsurprisingly, Blacklock's essay was not a best-seller, but while few people were aware of his views, I found his words

---

[3]*Encyclopaedia Britannica* 1775. Blindness entry written by Dr Thomas Blacklock – 1st edition. Cambridge University Library.

comforting. In a time where blind people were mostly ignored, hidden at home or in institutions, and were a collective group who rarely had a voice about themselves or their treatment, his notion that blind people should be educated so they could have a role in society was a refreshing idea. This became far more prominent in the nineteenth century, and it is heartening that Blacklock fought in the blind person's corner at a time when few had a voice.

A hundred years after Blacklock's definitions, the social writer Samuel Smiles wrote his best-selling book *Self-help*, which showed, through case studies, the Victorian values of thrift, industry and progress. This ethos promoted how self-sufficiency could lead to higher spiritual value and internal beauty, particularly for the 'misfortunate' blind. The South London Association for Assisting the Blind, for example, echoed such thinking in their annual report of 1844, where they declared their aim was 'to help the poor blind to help themselves'. In their general notes it was argued:

> *... their training and education as intelligent beings is incumbent on the community and when it is seen that in so many cases their labor may be productive and assist materially towards their maintenance, it becomes not only*

a duty, but an economic advantage to the country that all should receive proper attention.[4]

Toward the end of the nineteenth century, asylums, charities and institutions proliferated and became increasingly professionalized in order to fulfil this economic push.[5]

*   *   *

Perhaps even more pertinently for me, the nineteenth century also gave birth to a remarkable group of influential and educated blind people. They found, through education and access to influential leaders, the ability to voice their own concerns, both as individuals or as a collective group, and demanded that blind people, and their education, should be part of society. Whether this was by schooling, reading, or working and earning money was not always clear, but within one hundred years of Blacklock's declarations, unions, charities and communities renewed their philosophy and showed that, via small steps, blind people had found a way to own their own lives, on their

---

[4]Bartley, G. C. *The Schools for the People containing the History, Development of English School for the Industrial and Poorer Classes* (London, 1871), p. 352.
[5]Phillips, *The Blind in British Society*, p. 6.

own terms. While these voices were frequently ignored by sighted leaders, the drive was there.

While many monasteries and abbeys had educated blind people for centuries, the first formal school for 'the blind', the *Institut des Jeunes Aveugles* (Institute for Blind Youth) and its history have become legendary. Founded by Monsieur Valentin Haüy, a linguist and teacher, the story goes that Haüy stopped for lunch at Café des Aveugles (Blind Cafe) in 1771 on the Place de la Concorde, Paris. Here he witnessed a group of ten blind people from the local hospice being mocked by onlookers. Some were dressed in dunce's caps, some were wearing cardboard cut-out glasses, and one conducted an orchestra he could not see. Haüy was horrified at the degradation. The French historian Zina Weygand translated his memoir:

> *Wearing grotesque robes, dunce's caps and huge pasteboard spectacles, devoid of lenses, their music sheets turned away from them, they were forced to make a living by scraping crude bows across rough string instruments for the amusement of the crowd.*[6]

---

[6]Weygand, Zina. *The Blind in French Society from the Middle Ages to the Century of Louis Braille* (Stanford University Press, 2009), p. 91.

Such a spectacle was not novel in the streets of Paris. Blind people had frequently been part of a tradition of playing clumsy fools who would instantly make an audience laugh, echoing plays from medieval times. As he walked home, Haüy became determined to 'pull them [the blind] from the depths of darkness' and help integrate them into the sighted life of the city. In a bid to help blind people earn a more dignified livelihood, he declared he would start a school that would provide both academic and vocational training, with particular emphasis on the cultivation of texts with raised letters to read and on encouraging musical talent.

In a request for funds, dated November 1784 and addressed to the Philanthropic Society of Paris, he argued that 'at this very moment we are working on a project to make these unfortunate people useful to society while assuring them a means of subsistence'. The Royal Academy of Music in Paris also played concerts to raise money, as did the Academy of Sciences, by printing and selling Haüy's 1786 essay, 'An Essay on the Education of the Blind'. By December 1786, the *Institut des Jeunes Aveugles* had been inaugurated on Rue Notre-Dame des Victoires, Paris.

Starting as a day school (though ultimately moving to a residential establishment), Haüy's school offered a strict regime of classes, exercises and manual skills workshops to ensure a blind child would be a culturally aware and contributing citizen. Aged between five and twelve, students were taught maths, spelling, geography, languages and, using raised letters, reading and music. There were also vocational workshops for children over twelve, where crafts such as carpentry and spinning were taught. Haüy also wanted children to learn how to use the letterpress he had invented. Students were taught typography and book binding. Once a child had mastered the method, it was then their duty to teach other new students. Owing to the slow process of making them, the books available were few, such as the gospels. Both rich and poor were taught together.

Other institutions followed suit and many European pedagogues followed Haüy's template and used his school as a model. Schools opened across France, with teachers coming to Paris to learn the skills that they would take back to their rural towns. While Haüy was not able to remain director of the Paris institute throughout his life (his political leanings resulted in him being chased out of Paris), he moved on to start a school for the blind in St Petersburg for Alexander the Great. The French school flourished and continued under a variety of directors who carried Haüy's didactic flame forwards.

Reading the Haüy legend in many ways gave me great pleasure and hope. The call for blind people to have access to culture and knowledge was not just a twenty-first-century battle cry; like finding out about Nandy the Neanderthal, it was a wave from the past that reminded me humans had been dealing with blindness forever. As I told my sister, I suspect I would have preferred, if given a choice, to be sent to a Parisian institution on the basis I might have been happier than in Vinton in the middle of the Midwest, as the education was very much more intellectual and cultural than that offered in the UK or United States.

While my French dream held steady for a while, it also still saddened me to hear all these stories through the voices of the sighted philanthropists and educators who created these institutions, rather than the blind students themselves. Where were they? And surely, they had a voice too?

* * *

The good news was that not only did blind people have a voice, but as the century wore on, they were voices that were heard and from all walks of life. There were also women's voices, such as one of my heroines, the educated and articulate Thérèse-Adèle Husson. Born in 1803, she attended and graduated from the Quinze-Vingts school and became a writer of children's books and romantic fiction before dying in 1831 in a house fire. While she left the legacy of her books, she also left her notebooks, which had a feisty private manifesto asking for a place at the over-subscribed institute.

While researching in the archives of the school in 2001, two eminent historians – Professor Cathy Kudlick and Professor Zina Weygand – found a medium-size notebook, eight by six inches, which contained eighty-three handwritten pages 'seemingly unmarked by time'.[7] The notes were entitled, simply, 'Reflections on the Physical and Moral Condition of the Blind by Mlle Adèle Husson, young blind woman of Nancy', and were composed as a series of chapters. The notes, dictated in the form of a letter, did not offer a well-thought-out political message.

Instead, she challenged, albeit inconsistently and often quite petulantly, a presumed identity of blind women in the nineteenth century. In describing the gait and walk of a blind person, for example, Adèle challenged the perceived

---

[7]Weygand, Zina, and Kudlick, Catherine. *Reflections: The Life and Writings of a Young Blind Woman in Post-revolutionary France* (NYU Press, 2002), p. 9.

character of blindness: 'While blind people's mobility is often "uncertain and trembling", this is not a blind person's intrinsic nature – more a consequence of not seeing.' She should join the Quinze-Vingts institution because, she argues, it was the sighted who imposed their fantasies of the blind on the blind, and the blind people should challenge this. Such words confirmed that she understood sighted people considered 'the blind' vacant and passive. Adèle was clear: blind people, given the right tools and education, could be self-aware, active and self-determined.

Adèle's notes were not just a request to join a blind community, but as Professors Weygand and Kudlick proved, were also the voice of a serious woman with her own agency. Adèle showed the use of a vocabulary and idealism that proved she knew about persuasion. She had opinions on almost every topic, including marriage (blind people should not marry, she claims, despite the fact she married later in her own life) and how people should dress (luxuriously if funds allow). She even mulls over how blind women are just as vain as sighted women.

> *Since I've promised to speak sincerely, I should also add that a certain degree of coquettishness also enters into how we carry ourselves, and here I speak only of female companions of misfortune. When we are confident enough*

to be clothed in a pretty dress and dainty shoes, decked out in these luxurious things ... we're so worried about how we might look ... We thus inspire tender emotions as people console us, feel sorry for us, when in fact they should be punishing our pride.[8]

Adèle was not the only blind woman finding her voice in the nineteenth century; over in Victorian Britain another blind woman was also declaring her views, this time in the public arena: the more famous (in the London literary salons) Mrs Hippolyte van Lendegem. Mrs Lendegem used her platform to question the nineteenth-century perception of blind people and in particular their education. Writing in her autobiography, she argued for the end of segregating children away from mainstream society and that society used blindness to construct a 'prison' around blind people. Without stimulus, Lendegem argued, blind people were left in a vacuum. Biography was, of course, a very useful way through which people could experience the lives of others, and certainly became increasingly fashionable in the mid-to-late nineteenth century.

What I love most about these women is that they challenged the mythologizing of blind people – either as

---

[8]Weygand and Kudlick, *Reflections*, p. 9.

gods or saints, or vacant drunks and beggars; broken objects to be fixed, or subjects of intellectual and scientific debate. Instead, they were individuals – a group who had desires and dreams like the rest of humanity. And while this was a relief in some ways – to know that my own access to education had come from the call by other blind and visually impaired women – it was sad to find so few from the hillsides of history.

* * *

We should be acting unwisely, if, in giving alms to the blind, we took them out of society and snapped the cord which binds them to society. I dread making recluses of them [the blind] for life, or for any long period, and though such a course may have been adopted out of pious and benevolent motives, I think it is a mischievous mistake.

WILLIAM GLADSTONE, Prime Minister
Speech attending the General Welfare Association, 1863

Beyond France's borders, the call for blind people to be educated also began to grow, with missionaries even being sent to China. Over in Britain, around the time Haüy was forming his school, the blind poet Edward Rushton founded the prestigious School for the Indigent Blind in

Liverpool in 1791.[9] Two years later, a similar school started in Edinburgh. By 1820, there were institutions of various sizes from Dublin to Munich, Rome and Zurich. In the United States, in 1829, the New England Asylum for the Blind, near Boston, was founded by Gridley Howe, and in 1852 Vinton, the school I visited with my sister, opened. The era of educating the blind in institutions with their own private system of governance and teaching methods had begun.

Interestingly, the British and subsequently the US systems, such as the school at Vinton, focused far more on vocational and manual training rather than the shared intellectual and cultural life espoused by the French. The ethos leaned heavily on skills for work, and trained students as weavers, ironmongers, locksmiths, organ blowers and tool sharpeners.[10] Many institutions offered only industrial training, providing instruction in particular skills such as brush and basket making. With help from public subscriptions, petitions and powerful patrons (including Queen Victoria), projects were created for the blind populace with the clear intention of adding to the stock of

---

[9]Royden, W. Michael. *Pioneers and Perseverance: A History of the Royal School for the Blind, Liverpool, 1791–1991* (Countyvise Ltd, Liverpool, 1991), p. 11.
[10]Lees, Colin, and Ralph, Sue. 'Charitable provision for blind people and deaf people in late 19th-century London.' *Journal of Research in Special Educational Needs*, 4(3) (2004): 148–60.

economic and moral wealth of the Empire and society. The blind student had to be able to create their own self-sufficiency and self-improvement.

Even when philanthropy had a more mainstream status by the 1840s and 1850s, such as the school we visited in Vinton, charities and institutions demanded inmates/pupils and pensioners must be responsible for their own futures. Blindness, for all the pity it inspired, was not a reason to be morally lax or dependent on society. By the 1830s there were over five hundred schools and charities for 'the blind' in Great Britain, including highly regarded ones in London, Liverpool, Edinburgh and Glasgow. By the end of the 1880s, over thirty-two charities for the blind existed in London alone. Satellite charities grew up in major cities including Manchester, Newcastle and Leeds. Blindness, more than other disabilities, it would seem, was slowly becoming part of mainstream society's need to improve itself.

*　*　*

I wish to ensure a blind workman a fixed sum weekly, in remuneration for his labor, and also to teach those too old for admission into some institutions, some trade.[11]
ELISABETH GILBERT in a letter to Queen Victoria

---
[11] Phillips, *The Blind in British Society*, pp. 95–6.

As you would imagine in nineteenth-century Britain, most of the drive around such charitable thinking came from privileged white men, who used their wealth, status and position in society to influence and change.

But what was also cheering for me was to discover these characters existed, and that a few well-educated blind advocates – such as Alexander Mitchell, Thomas Rhodes Armitage and John Bird (who would go on to found what is now known as the Royal National Institute of Blind People (RNIB)) – began to campaign for the collective opinion of their blind brethren and sisters. They, like their sighted counterparts, wished to help blind people as a collective identity, rather than a group of presumed vagabonds and layabouts. Their projects, along with a few others, revealed that not only had blind people begun to have a collective identity of their own, but also played their part in the sighted economic market.

Interestingly, blind people were mainly self-interested; they were not so concerned with other disabled groups, such as the deaf community. By 1900, they were instrumental in the creation of the National League of the Blind, an association that began to speak on and for the blind. They questioned whether putting a blind person in an institution engendered a collective identity of another sort and called for alternatives. The *Cornhill Magazine* also took up the call of criticizing the bad and erratic quality of blind education.

One of the most active new voices of this group, and possibly my favourite, was a young blind woman called Elizabeth Gilbert. 'Bessie', as her father referred to her, started, funded and continuously supported the clumsily named 'Association for Promoting the General Welfare of the Blind'. It later became known as the General Welfare Association and carried on into the twenty-first century as Clarity. Founded and based in London's Holborn district in 1854, the General Welfare Association was like other charities of the age, in that it was run as a subscription charity, and had amongst its subscribers Queen Victoria and Prime Minister William Gladstone.[12]

I think I identified with Bessie because, like me, she had more advantages than most and had an excellent education, given she was the second daughter of the Master of Brasenose College, Oxford University. As did many children of the era, Bessie contracted scarlet fever aged three, which resulted in the complete loss of her eyesight and serious scarring to her throat. While specialists confirmed her eyesight was destroyed, the advice of a leading London oculist was to take her home and treat her the same as her

---

[12] Phillips, *The Blind in British Society*, p. 117.

other eleven sighted sisters and brothers. Her parents took such instructions to heart. She had to find her own place at table, dress herself and walk around the garden unaided. My parents would have been proud.

Her parents also encouraged her to talk, interact and dine with her father's guests, who were some of the leading intellectuals, thinkers, philanthropists and poets of the day, including Thomas De Quincey and William Wordsworth. According to Elizabeth's sister, Wordsworth stayed with the family when she was ten years old, on his way to receiving his honorary doctorate. Aside from sharing a love of nature with her (they apparently discussed birds and flowers throughout the stay), he once walked into the drawing room and, on seeing her, declared in a deep gloomy tone, 'Madam! I hope I do not disturb you!' and walked out. As she wrote to her sister, she held his 'madam' close to her youthful heart for many years.[13]

Yet regardless of her privileged upbringing, by the time she was twenty-five, Bessie knew her choices in nineteenth-century society were limited. She bemoaned in a letter to her father that marriage was not an option for her and that she was required to take on the role of spinster aunt with

---

[13]Martin, Frances. *Elizabeth Gilbert and her Work for the Blind* (Macmillan, New York, 1923).

some charitable enterprise to occupy her. This would have been the status for most privileged blind ladies. But Bessie was not inclined to disappear quietly. In a bid to find out more about education for 'the blind', she wrote to a family friend, William Hank Levy. Levy was a young blind teacher at the school for the blind in St John's Wood, London, and she asked him to investigate by what means his students survived after their schooling.

In a working partnership that would last for the rest of their lives, Levy reported back with shocking news. Despite the goodwill and funding, the reality he found was that blind schooling in Britain was in disarray. Most of the schools did not co-operate or help each other. Each school seemed to have a particular bias, learning method and different policies around blindness. They all jostled against each other for position and funds. Moreover, many of these were supposed to be judged only by need and suitability. Instead, they were partial and narrow, particularly if a candidate could not prove their religion or provenance. It seemed almost a lottery as to who might gain a place.

Secondly, even when students were accepted, sighted instructors were badly trained and did not understand the sensory needs of their students. Most could not use the specialist reading inventions. Worse still, schools did not nurture blind people like Bessie herself – educated, economically independent and desiring to be part of the sighted community. If anything, they discouraged independence. Through Levy's enquiries, they discovered there was little preparation for blind people to lead a life as part of the sighted world. There was little or no equipment in terms of trades and skills for the outside world, and there was almost no help at all for those who became blind later on in life. There was no retraining, no schooling or housing. Most blind adult men were destitute and reliant on begging; the fate of most women was unknown.

On the back of this report, in May 1854, Bessie started a new project that she hoped would ameliorate such issues. With the support of her father, she wrote to Queen Victoria in January 1856 and received patronage. The aim of her project was 'to make blind men self-sufficient through provision of a trade they could train', sell themselves and earn a living. The trade, she decided, would be basket making, and she set up a depository of basic materials to help blind weavers in a warehouse in London's Holborn district. According to her letters asking for backing, her idea was to provide and supply the men (and later women) with the materials required to make something that could be sold on the open market. If necessary, she insisted, the charity would buy and finish the items and sell them on. A student from the St John's Wood School for the Blind was contracted to dye the baskets. After baskets came brushes, doormats, chair caning, boxing and carpentry. While for two years the project ran at a loss, by 1856 the public had taken up the cause. Many sponsored workers. Others, such as Queen Victoria and the prime minister, William Gladstone, helped via financial subscription. Because of such funding, along with the actual profits, the charity was soon able to rent a shop and warehouse to allow direct sales to the public.

This was the first organization of its kind and was admired by sighted and blind alike. Indeed, it was arguably one of the most publicized and most approved blind agencies of the era. By 1857, the enterprise was so big that Bessie founded a committee of management. Two years later, it was engaged in nineteen different trades. Possibly because the two original architects of the project, Gilbert and Levy, were blind themselves, the General Welfare Association had a strong identity not only with their blind fellows but also the sighted community.

The Association also supported its workers in more ways than simply providing work. There was a lending library of embossed books and it instigated reading lessons. There was better pay for the teachers and guides. In later years, it also incorporated a musical society for the blind, of which William Hank Levy was a founding member, and put on fundraising concerts and lessons for members. Its template spread further afield; it bought its own boarding house, so blind people could come into London to be trained in a skill and then return to the rural community with a trade.

Above all, while Bessie's projects were not designed to replace institutions, being founded on the 'self-sufficient' principles that dominated the century, they also proved the Malthusian theory wrong: blind people could support themselves and not be a burden. With help from public subscriptions, petitions and powerful patrons, these blind pioneers created workshops, home teaching groups and co-operatives, with the clear intention of granting blind people a means to create 'remunerative labour', as every good empire builder should do. Their precise intention was to grant people a means to support themselves and to be part of society.

I suppose, having understood this was an age of great self-sufficiency, it is possible to imagine that the General Welfare Association would have existed whether Bessie started it or not. Her charity was the perfect expression of the age, and was similar to other self-sustaining charities, such as the quaintly named Guild of the Brave Poor Things, a charity started and run by young disabled men, whose emblem was a sword crossed with a crutch.

* * *

Perhaps why I connect with Bessie is not only because she was a trusted conduit through which blind people could find a voice, but also because she had the unique experience of having the backing of a family who treated her no differently from her siblings and gave her a mainstream education. From the beginning of her life, she was granted her own status in the community. And while it is true that the General Welfare Association provided simple, manual occupations, which today would be menial, repetitive and patronizing, it was a unique enterprise for its time. It put the idea in the public's mind that a blind person could live amongst a family and contribute to it with a living wage, rather than being entirely reliant on institutions or charity.

While there would be different views and while no exact solutions emerged about what would best help 'the blind', Bessie and others showed for the first time that blindness had been considered part of mainstream society and that the blind themselves were part of the decision-making process. Indeed, the education of every blind person, poor or prosperous, would not be fully addressed in any wider sense until the late nineteenth century and beyond. Bessie, Adèle and Hippolyte proved that not only could blind people challenge conventional notions about blind people, they could also challenge our notions of the past.

* * *

As much as I was cheered by Adèle, Bessie and other amazing blind women, the truth is that for the majority of blind people, being blind in nineteenth-century Europe was not an easy fate, usually resulting in poverty, isolation and mistreatment.

While education and access to knowledge (to the sighted at least) became key in helping blind people, the question of what such 'educated' students should do after they finished school continued. Where would they go? Could they get work? Would they have to simply move to another workhouse or asylum of some kind? Or, as in centuries past, would they be forced to return to begging? As the era wore on, increasing numbers of blind adults, including the lucky few who had been educated, found themselves destitute again and applying for what few places existed in blind hospices for adults and the aged. While the existence of schools meant the material condition of young people was improved, it was not clear how adulthood could be managed.

It was a question the British, during their booming Industrial Revolution, engaged with on a widespread scale. While previous Poor Laws from 1601 had demanded local parishes should specifically care for the sick, lame, deaf and blind, such a safety net – if it can be called that – meant that cottage-based agricultural families could supplement their food and income based on a blind aunt, grandmother, brother, sister or husband.

Owing to the new poor laws of 1834, this help was now completely withdrawn. Instead, large-scale factories provided work for the able that relied on wages which were calculated per head. Such meagre earnings could not provide for non-earning family members. Now a blind relative was one more mouth to feed. Because they did not fulfil the 'able' category and were thus unable to contribute to the economic wealth of the Empire, the only option for families with blind offspring was to hopefully send them to the blind schools that were opening across the country.

The consequence of the new Acts and its classification of the human condition made an already difficult situation worse. For many, unless they had learnt a skill when sighted, the world of repetitive self-acting machines, fast-moving vehicles and carriages and constantly changing gadgetry was terrifying. The Acts clearly defined those who were 'able-bodied' and those who were not. This category was in turn subdivided into the 'impotent poor' and the 'aged poor', the deserving and undeserving.

They also distinguished between the 'able' and the 'unable', or as was increasingly used, the 'disabled' – the term which we still use today. The new laws mandated that those who could not support themselves for whatever reason were 'undeserving' and must now commit to the newly created 'workhouses'. All poor relief, previously supplied by local churches, must now be discouraged, and all itinerant and poor blind people were to be sent to the poor house.

Workhouses were not new. Reported as far back as 1388, they were originally invented as places to address labour shortages after the Black Death and they housed the destitute of the local parish. Yet the nineteenth-century version was a terrifying place. These beacons of so-called civility were purposefully created to be unforgiving and incarcerating, run by Poor Law Authorities that hoped to profit from the free labour of their inmates. Such places caused immeasurable suffering, poverty and malnourishment. Those who refused to go often starved to death. Outcries in *The Times* newspaper continually pointed out the desperate conditions its inmates lived in, with writers such as Charles Dickens and Wilkie Collins also voicing deep concern.

So alongside the massive boom in Victorian philanthropy, doing good and the rise of schooling for blind students, social understanding and the parallel implementation of the law meant blind people were still exiled from mainstream society. Occasionally, they could try to find work that did not demand sight and were helped by their blind compatriots. But for many, the age-old profession of begging on the highways remained the only alternative.

*   *   *

As the nineteenth century ended, blindness (and other misfortunes) allowed the sighted world to wave philanthropic flags and build charitable institutions. The strong theme across Europe and the United States was one in which blind people began to gain a strong new collective identity and be the masters (or mistresses) of their own fate.

Yet, despite the high level of recruitment into charities, their success was not only an indication of the blooming philanthropic spirit and social improvement drive; it was also a sign that society was keen to release itself from the burden of having to engage with blindness. While previous eras had certainly segregated the blind by either tainting them as an amorphous group of itinerant beggars or as medical objects of interest, nineteenth-century society continued the segregation tradition – blindness being 'a lack' that required reparations. Moreover, it was now a state where the person blinded (whether since birth or during life) became responsible for their treatment and their role in society. Such a responsibility was heavy, lightened only occasionally by innovative and compassionate advocates. In other words, blindness had shifted from a state that could be cured to a state of personal tragedy which had to be supported, by one means or another. It is a view, I would argue, that persists today.

* * *

I think what my visit to the blind school at Vinton, and then my further exploration into blind educational establishments, showed me is that so much of how you cope with your life is dependent on choices that you have little control over.

This can be the world you are born into, the access to wealth along the road, and even the accidents, wars and diseases that come into your life. So much depends on how you find the energy to fight for what you want. Do you thrive because of your nature or how you were nurtured? Are you more prone to feeling down and depressed about your blindness if everyone tells you it is the worst thing that can happen to you? Or do you revolt and fight back, and prove the bastards (the naysayers) wrong? Do you give up if your teachers insist you are stupid, but it turns out years later it was not for lack of intelligence that you did not understand mathematics, but the fact you could not see the whiteboard with any of the markings on it and were too embarrassed to ask for help (which is what happened to me)?

I am sure some will answer how people cope with sight loss is no different from how we deal with any vicissitude we come upon, blind or not. But I have pondered, given how the modern world is so dependent on the visual, whether perhaps you need a certain aptitude and confidence to navigate not only the real physical objects in your way, but the psychological challenges too.

Blindness, as we have discovered in past chapters, is assumed to have a devastating impact upon people, young or old, and how you cope with this great drama is also how the world perceives even the concept of blindness.

For me, perhaps knowing that others have struggled with definitions, constructs, and the fears too, has helped me feel less alone. Above all, I am rather grateful for my parents' decision, almost with a Dunkirk mindset, to force me to engage with the world on my own terms. It might have made engaging with my limits a bit harder, but it certainly gave me the courage to live the life I chose. Which I do, and always will.

6

Reading it

Pure fiction

His countenance reminded one of a lamp quenched, waiting to be relit and alas it was not himself that could now kindle the lustre of animated expression; he was dependent upon another.[1]

The nineteenth-century notion of blindness was not all about the Industrial Revolution, charity and philanthropy.

Another thread that kept blindness and blind people very much in the mainstream consciousness (albeit with negative connotations) was the use, yet again, of blind people as markers and characters in novels, plays and memoirs. No longer the static, mythical blind heroes of classical and medieval literature, blind people were now useful plot devices to denote difference and show the vicissitudes and drama of life.

---

[1] Brontë, Charlotte. *Jane Eyre* (Norton Critical Edition, 1988).

As many literary commentators have pointed out, a 'blind character' is a useful narrative device to express conversion, curing and horror, and thus the perfect plot device to create melodrama. Blindness created a subtle tension in fiction as it provided a useful mechanism to move the plot on. Blindness could also act as the perfect metaphor to represent evil, innocence, truth, tension, fear and danger, rather than allow characters to have emotions.

Perhaps not so surprisingly, given we all know he wrote about the disabled Tiny Tim in *A Christmas Carol*, Charles Dickens was one of the main nineteenth-century authors to use the presumed blind gloom trope, both in fiction and non-fiction. In the opening of his travelogue from the United States in 1842, *Notes from America*, he rushes to Boston to interview a young blind, deaf and nonspeaking woman called Laura Bridgeman, who could only communicate by means of finger typing on another human's hands. Dickens, who did not enjoy his time in the United States, ended his journal by noting that there were two highlights of his tour: one was seeing Niagara Falls, the other was meeting Laura Bridgeman. His description of her makes for uneasy reading.

There she was before me; built up as it were in a marble cell, impervious to any ray of light or particle of sound; with her poor white hand peeking through a chink in the wall, beckoning to some good man for help, that an immortal soul might be awakened.[2]

Dickens was not the first person to write about Laura Bridgeman. When he met her in 1842, she was already a national celebrity. Born in New Hampshire in 1829 to hard-working farm folk, Laura lost her vision and hearing aged two from scarlet fever. Offered a free place in 1837 at the New England Asylum for the Blind (now the Perkins Institute for the Blind), she was proudly presented to the funders of the institute and the local press as an 'angel soul'. Here was the nineteenth-century emblem who embodied education, self-sufficiency and charitable provision in action. Even Helen Keller argued that her own life would not have been possible without her. Dickens was merely one of 10,000 visitors that queued at Perkins to see this 'triumph'. Even Queen Victoria asked after Laura's health.

---

[2]Dickens, Charles. *Notes from America – The Blind* (Chapman and Hall, London, 1891), p. 26.

Dickens also used blind characters in his fiction, particularly in his short novella *The Cricket in the Hearth* (1845). Written for the Christmas season, the 'quiet and domestic' fairy story, which was often published in the same volume as *A Christmas Carol,* follows the usual template of melodrama, conflict, misunderstandings, crisis and happy sentimental resolution. Dickens, who performed the story live on stage, wrote a classic tale of redemption and love. It is the story of May and Edward, whose obstacle to marriage is social status (he is beneath her well-to-do world). It is also the story of a much wealthier catch, the evil Mr Tackleton. May's best friend Dot, who is happily married to John, wants the same for her friend, and spends most of the story trying to reunite the loving couple, albeit with a few misunderstandings on the way. By the end of the merry dance, everyone is happy.

Along the way, however, we also hear the story of Edward's blind sister, Bertha, who has dreams and desires of her own, all unfulfilled. Instead, she is referred to by her father as 'poor blind Bertha' (thank God blind Bertha's name provided an opportunity for alliteration – at least she had that) and her home life, he tells May, is set up so she does not see the 'hardships' of life. Bertha will never belong to the world of courtship and marriage, or even 'overcoming' her adversity. She cannot be cured by doctors, or by love – and thus cannot be a heroine in her own right.

Dickens is clearly a product of his age, and his short stories show how his readership wanted redemption narratives. He constructs a tale brilliantly; we all know that there will be a beginning, middle and end, and the end must end happily – but with Dickens the journey and the characters are the treat. And for those of us who indulge in reading Victorian novels as a pastime, we also know that melodrama is about emotions and the creation of scenes to heighten these emotions.

Over in France, Charles Baudelaire, the acclaimed poet, also couched blindness in the 'terrible loss' category. Take, for instance, this poem from *The Flowers of Evil (Les Fleurs du Mal)* in 1857. The mention of 'them', the blind, are *'vraiment affreux'* (truly frightful) and *'pareils aux mannequins'* (like mannequins), their eyes *'d'où la divine étincelle est partie'* (from which the divine spark has departed). I quote the poem here to give you the full hopelessness.

> *Contemplate them, my soul; they are truly frightful!*
> *Like mannequins; vaguely ridiculous;*
> *Strange and terrible, like somnambulists;*

Darting, one never knows where, their tenebrous orbs.
Their eyes, from which the divine spark has departed,
Remain raised to the sky, as if they were looking
Into space: one never sees them toward the pavement
Dreamily bend their heavy heads.[3]

The sense of a blind person having no chance in life – despite education, the development of Braille and employment factories for blind people – still permeated nineteenth-century European life, and continued to ratify the idea that to lose one's sight was the worst thing possible.

So even from a casual survey of these nineteenth-century novelists and poets, we can follow how they milked the blind cow. They knew how to represent blindness in an emotional way, far more than simply as a person gaining education and self-sufficiency. Because blindness is not as visible as other disabilities, writers would often mix it with other bodily differences such as dwarfism or lameness; this heightened a spectator's smug knowledge between 'normal' and the 'blind', reminding the viewer they remained on the 'safer' spectator side of the room or page. In other words, it reassured an audience that they were 'normal'.

---

[3]Baudelaire, Charles. 'The Blind'. PoetryVerse, translated by William Aggeler.

As the academic Leonard Davis has pointed out, this is not really that helpful for a woman hoping for a full and rich life – with sight or not. It told me that I could never attain the status of heroine in my own life. Silly Selina.

* * *

If Dickens and Baudelaire can be forgiven for distilling and perpetuating the myth of the blind inspirational innocent, so too can other nineteenth-century writers. Charlotte Brontë's *Jane Eyre* is a case in point. It's fair to say that the story of the clever, vibrant and witty governess has always emboldened me. Here was a female character who knew her own mind and was not swayed by status or money to remove her from her dreary life. Jane Eyre always spoke to me in very modern terms.

As someone losing her sight, however, on rereading the novel, I do find my relationship to the plot and its outcome has shifted; the theme of seeing and not seeing, of being recognized and not being recognized, is far more pertinent throughout the novel than I first remember. It is stuffed with references to what people see and what they don't, and our heroine herself is constantly watching and being watched, and not being recognized for her true self. Above all, the hero of the story, Mr Rochester, is only redeemed and allowed to be loved when he is blind. He only regains part of his sight once he has paid the price for his wicked ways. The blind allegory appears, again and again, to act as a means of another sighted character saving the blind one.

The plot is well known. Jane Eyre becomes the governess to a young girl at the stately home of Mr Rochester, and during her stay they fall in love and plan to marry. But on the day of the wedding, their love is thwarted as a first wife is discovered in the attic, mentally ill and violent. By the end of the novel we are told a major fire has burnt down Thornfield and killed or maimed its occupants. When Jane sees her beloved Rochester again after the fire, she spies on him first, to see what state he is in. Once he knows it is her, he declares his blind life is 'dark, dreary, hopeless' and that he is

> *doing nothing, expecting nothing, merging night into day; feeling nothing but the sensation of cold when I let the fire go out, hunger when I forget to eat.*[4]

Other than losing Jane, blindness, he says, is the worst thing that could have happened to him, and one presumes nineteenth-century readers would agree.

---

[4] Brontë, *Jane Eyre*.

Yet again, we are being told to tap into the pity of blindness (echoing for us of the biblical Sampson being blinded); here is a strong, dominant Rochester (without his beloved Jane), but blindness has taken away his strength. With echoes of Oedipus from classical antiquity, and even the conversion of Saul to Paul, Rochester's blindness renders him entirely helpless, and thus destroyed.

Her return provides a tense denouement: will she accept her man, even blind? Will he accept her, and accept her care? Reader, as we know, she marries Rochester, and he even gains a small amount of sight back. He is redeemed through love. Blindness is overcome, thank goodness.

To give Charlotte Brontë some credit, it seems that Jane is smart and thoughtful enough to know, whether blind or not, Rochester is Rochester. The lines in which she accepts his love, despite his own misgivings of simply being her beloved, are perfection. 'Am I hideous Jane?' he asks her. 'Very sir. You always were, you know.' She is 'bone of his bone' and 'flesh of his flesh', however blind and impaired he is. But I do wonder, in a little flirtation with fantasy: if my husband had met me earlier, according to these rules, would I have regained my sight? Dear reader, I married him *and* still have little vision.

* * *

Not all nineteenth-century melodrama obeyed the redemption or tragedy template of blindness. A surprisingly more liberating state of blindness is portrayed in a novel entitled *Poor Miss Finch* (1872) by Wilkie Collins. Collins, known best for what is often cited as the first detective novel, *The Moonstone*, and the thriller *The Woman in White*, was a close friend of Dickens, and they often collaborated and shared publishers. When I first discovered the novel, I presumed he would follow Dickens's suit and use blindness as a melodramatic plot line. To some degree he does, but in an intriguing way.

For the uninitiated, *Poor Miss Finch*[5] revolves around the love and life of Lucilla Finch, the wealthy blind daughter of a rector in the satirically named Dimchurch in Sussex. As the book begins, she is joined by a new paid companion, the charming and rather silly Madame Pratolungo ('long-winded' in Italian). Lucilla is a lively soul who has fallen in love with her wealthy neighbour, Mr Oscar Dubourg. All seems well, until Oscar has an accident and needs nursing (which Lucilla does well). This comes at the same time as the arrival of his evil twin brother, Nugent, who has spent

---

[5]Collins, Wilkie. *Poor Miss Finch*. Ed. Catherine Peters (Oxford University Press, 2000 (1872)).

his entire inheritance in the United States while learning to be a painter.

In what might have been a simple and loving courtship, the two brothers wrestle over the affections of Miss Finch. She has an operation, regains her eyesight, and is courted and trapped by the debt-ridden brother who, as all twins do, presents himself as the good brother, Oscar. Happily, Madame Pratolungo, who is not as stupid as she first seemed, finds the good twin, and together they rescue Miss Finch. By by the end of the novel, Miss Finch has lost her sight again, perhaps because the operation does not work and perhaps from the trauma of the drama. Unusually for a nineteenth-century novel, she does not care and becomes emancipated. Her sight is not saved, but she has the love of her life, Oscar. Love is stronger than sight, the novel seems to say, even though the story is a bit of a farce.

What is comforting about this story is that Collins presents blindness not only as a device through which to explore emotion, but also a state which can be lived with and chosen. Collins, as much as he knows all the melodramatic buttons to press for his Victorian audience, uses blindness as a useful part of the chief protagonist's life and makes the title of the book, *Poor Miss Finch*, as ironic as the character portrayed.

Given that authors have the right to place their characters as they see fit, the theme that binds all these stories together – and that readers will naturally understand and accept – is how blindness is presumed a disadvantage and disempowerment. Laura Bridgeman, Bertha in *The Cricket in the Hearth*, Mr Rochester in *Jane Eyre* and Miss Finch in Collins's parody are moral signposts. Even Miss Finch must battle other people's preconceptions of blindness.

Somehow these representations, while fictional, re-emphasize the idea that sighted people have the right to live lives as they choose but that blind people do not. Sighted people get to choose who they marry, to have ambition, to love, but blind people do not. Worse still, it confirms the idea that a blind woman or man can never be the hero of a tale, and society ratifies this notion by telling us that blind people cannot have these dreams, or have the same potential as sighted people, because they are blind.

What I hated across all these tales was how there is always a definite sense of difference – 'them and us' – with the sighted reader safely on the side of the sighted and 'the blind' placed carefully in a different box, giving us a nice binary opposition of 'deformed' and 'normal'. As usual.

* * *

Perhaps the most unexpected genre to focus and represent blindness in more recent times is the post-apocalyptic or science fiction genre. While there is a plethora to choose from, from H. G. Wells to John Wyndham, and more recently José Saramago, what is intriguing is how blindness is still represented as a calamity, and one where the powerful are the people with sight. The plot lines all have similar themes, usually giving the superior position of power to sighted people, versus the enslaved blind people. Many early twentieth-century writers, having seen or foreseen the atrocities of disease and war, wrote about the fear of what could happen if blindness was to take over our lives.

H. G. Wells's short story 'The Country of the Blind' (1904),[6] for example, tells of a sighted mountaineer called Nunez, who finds himself in a much heard of, but never found, 'Country of the Blind' in the valleys of Ecuador that has been isolated from the rest of the world for centuries. All the inhabitants, including the daughter of the leader, are blind from some ancient disease that affected their ancestors, and are depicted as happy and self-sufficient, as well as the

---

[6]Wells, H. G. 'The Country of the Blind', in *The Country of the Blind and Other Stories*. Ed. Michael Sherborne (Oxford University Press, 1996).

same old myth – having heightened other senses. At the same time, Nunez sees that they are also closed-minded and insular to the point of xenophobia – the implication being they can't see beyond their own world. He tries to explain to them, via the old proverb, 'In the Country of the Blind, the one-eyed man is King', but they do not understand the concept of sight, having not had it for generations. Instead, they allow him to stay on the condition he abides by their customs and ways of working, to which he agrees and settles in.

So Nunez remains in this 'Country of the Blind' and learns to adapt to a blind way of living, with no windows and easily marked pathways. He also falls in love with the leader's daughter; she shows him how to function in the Country of the Blind and he tries to explain to her the joys of sight. But when he decides to marry his love, the father, after consultation with the village, offers him a stark choice: if he wishes to marry her, he must be blinded. The morning of the operation to blind our hero arrives, and he must decide.

Without ruining the story, let us just say his choice is not easy, and does not end well. Surprisingly, in 1939 Wells wrote a different ending to the original version, which was published in a collection of his short stories, as there was much outcry at the first version. While I somewhat expected the rather imperialistic-sounding phrases by Nunez, such as his surprise at the 'astonishing cleanliness' and the 'order' of the blind village – and my favourite, 'These fools must be blind!' when he first spies them; 'It seemed they knew nothing of sight. No matter he would teach them' – the story ultimately emphasizes, yet again, how the sighted world is much superior to the blind one and that blindness is seen as state of loss and negativity. The fear from the story comes from the idea that a whole village and culture lives with blindness, and the hero (and the reader) is confronted with what to give up – the love of our life or our sight?

There are many other such sci-fi stories which use the 'horrifying' state of blindness to chill us. Most memorable is how the sighted also have the upper hand in John Wyndham's 1951 novel *The Day of the Triffids*.[7] Here we follow the protagonist Bill Masen, who wakes up bandaged and blind in a hospital in London and finds out that most people in the world have been blinded by an apparent meteor shower. Even worse, an aggressive species of plant starts to grow, and begins killing people. Through a series of adventures and escapes, he ends up in a sighted enclave in Sussex fighting off the monstrous triffids and hoping to join a

---

[7] Wyndham, John. *The Day of the Triffids* (Michael Joseph, 1951).

sighted haven on the Isle of Wight. Heaven forbid our hero is blind forever.

One more novel is also worth commenting on. One of Portugal's most famous writers, José Saramago, who won the Nobel Prize for literature, wrote his famous novel *Blindness*[8] in 1995, and it has subsequently been turned into a film and a play. It follows, like *The Day of the Triffids*, a virus that hits the world and blinds everyone. The government puts all the infected into quarantine blocks, and the power dynamics of blind people held by sighted people ensues. Yet again, blindness is shown as the worst event that can befall a person. It also shows how the sighted heroine (who fakes being blind) is the only means to allow the escape of the good blind people. Yes, it's true: blind people are quite a nasty bunch when imprisoned and treated badly.

*   *   *

Sadly, there are too many narratives about perpetuating the inspirational blind person to mention, so I hope the above gives you a glimpse of how we have been fed blind drama. Just one more blind author before we move on: the

---

[8]Saramago, José. *Blindness*. Translated by Giovanni Pontiero (Harvest Books, 1999).

blind and deaf author Helen Keller (1880–1968). Her work is a useful conduit to think about blind narratives, as her life and work straddle both the nineteenth and twentieth centuries. Keller's legacy, both in stories of her life and her amazing collections of writing, seems to still pervade our notion of blind people's lives.

I first really began to think about Helen Keller a few years ago. Quite by chance, I was asked to give a lecture around the subject of 'Blindness and Dreams'. As ever, I was frustrated that this continual 'them blind folk and us sighted folk' template meant the title of the lecture presumed that blind people had different dreams from the sighted world. I accepted the invitation and decided to discuss how complicated the subject of blindness was, let alone that of dreams. It amused me that Keller wrote about the subject herself, and so I included her in my talk.

The day of the lecture arrived, and I was greeted at the door by the vice-president, who was dressed in a scratchy green tweed jacket and was full of enthusiasm and courtesy. 'We are so thrilled to have you here,' he said, grabbing my arm and marching me to an old creaking stage, an ancient library lectern and an expectant audience. He introduced me with great gusto. 'Ladies and gentlemen,' he enthused, 'may I present Selina Mills from BBC Radio's *In Touch* programme. We are thrilled to have her here to talk about blindness and dreams.' Everyone clapped. And then he raised his hands for a pause. 'I would like to add she stands in the shadow of another great blind and deaf writer and thinker, Helen Keller, who gave a lecture to the Society in 1913 on this very stage.' I have to say, my mouth and white cane almost dropped to the floor, and I grabbed the lectern.

I took a deep breath and decided to clear up a few myths before I launched into 'Blindness and Dreams'. Helen Keller, I began, was indeed a phenomenal activist and campaigner for disabled people and a prolific writer. While she is sold to us as an emblem of triumph over adversity, her life was actually very difficult. Like many other women of her era, financial matters were often run and used by ambitious and greedy people around her to perpetuate the pervasive and accepted construct of what blindness meant to a late nineteenth-century audience: cloying, needy, a tragedy and a burden. Even her own notion of blindness was full of the prejudices of the day and possibly what we would consider unsavoury eugenic beliefs.[9] Helen's story was, I concluded, a far more human story than simply that of the inspirational rise of a disabled educated woman.

---

[9]Schuermann, Katie. 'Why Helen Keller Believed In Eradicating People With Disabilities'. *The Federalist*, 9 September 2019.

I drew myself up further and peered ferociously at the crowd. Not many people these days also realize that Helen held deeply left-wing socialist views, to the extent that the FBI put her on their watch list of communists in 1949. In 1933, when her book *How I Became a Socialist* was burned by Nazi youth, she wrote an open letter to the Student Body of Germany condemning censorship and prejudice. In addition, few people know that Helen Keller wrote to her publisher and asked to write about the horrors of Apartheid, but she was told quite firmly that only 'blindness sells' – her social justice did not. She also fought for women's suffrage, animal rights and labour rights. Never mind, too, that few of the stories around Helen report of how her 'teacher', Annie Sullivan, insisted on the crafting of a career that made the most money for them both (which was not necessarily what Helen wanted) and was said to direct the tone and subject matter of Helen's books.

Sadder still, few people knew how Helen fell deeply in love with Peter Fagan, a young Boston journalist, and how, if gossip and rumour are to be believed, Sullivan and her parents not only thwarted the love match, but prevented it, by lying to Helen (they told her he was dead).[10] They knew if Helen upped and married, their darling girl would stop

---

[10]'Helen Keller: A Love Affair'. American Foundation for the Blind blog, 21 August 2016.

milking the blind myth cow, which everyone benefited from. Somehow this reminded me of Maria Theresia von Paradis in the eighteenth century: if you stop being 'blind', with all its mythical sense and inspiration, suddenly the pension pot stops.

As to the subject of the lecture I was supposed to be delivering on 'Blindness and Dreams', it was a typical question Keller had been asked herself. She replied that she could not answer the question, because she believed that she experienced the world in her daily life as much as everyone else – including her travels, her family and her work – and her brain conceptualized and turned the experiences into dreams.

One person in the audience asked impatiently: 'But what about colour? Did she dream in colour? Do totally blind people see objects and faces in their dreams?' I replied that there is no direct answer to this as it depends on when one lost one's sight. If one does not grow up using colour or faces as a reference point, how would one know how to describe them? It also depends on *when* you lose your sight. Some blind people know and understand the experience of colour; some do not. Of course, I completely understood why he might ask such a question – a question that many sighted people ask; the problem is that every blind person explains it differently.

In more modern times, doctors have also researched the question. Many have shared the brain scans of people blind since birth while they are sleeping. It turns out that blind people have the same type of vision-related electrical activity in the brain during sleep and dreaming as people with eyesight. Scientists at Harvard even did a study with twins (one blind, one sighted), and found their dream scans to look exactly alike, with the same electrical activity in the brain. In other words, people born blind can experience visual sensations as much as sighted people while sleeping. It is only that blind people might have had different references and experiences with which to articulate these sensations. Dreams are dreams, and part of all animal activity.[11]

The fantasy that blind people's experiences are so different from sighted people's is exactly that, a fantasy, connected to the idea that blindness separates us from the sighted world. Yes, it is true that blind people can't see, and that they experience the world through touch, taste and sound. No, it is not true that all blind people have extra-special use of their senses, but they more than likely use them in a different way. As I found throughout history, blindness is mythologized across so many genres – history, poetry,

---

[11] https://www.sleepfoundation.org/dreams/can-blind-people-dream

fiction, film, and even in memoirs and autobiographies – it's hardly surprising Helen Keller and her blind dreams had become part of this. Even asking the question about blind people's dreams suggests there is a special difference that might give us special understanding of blindness. I am afraid to say, I told my almost disappointed audience, no such luck.

I found myself arguing that whatever we think about blindness and dreams, the hardest thing to reflect upon is that we are reliant on a myth and fantasy that is not accurate. I asked, as I still do now, dare we suggest that the legacy of Helen Keller, the darling of the world tours, has hurt blind people by not acknowledging the realities of a blind life? Many blind writers have distanced themselves from the Helen Keller blind myth. Superb blind writers, such as Ved Mehta, Aldous Huxley, Stephen Kuusisto, and more recently Georgina Kleege, have challenged and commented on the damage the chipper-blind memoir factory can cause.

Feeling emboldened, I finished my talk by reminding people of the reality of blind people's lives; how blind writers feel the burden of having to supply tales and dreams of happy blindness, with no fears, falls or anxiety, that comfort and set the template for sighted people for the modern era. One could even argue that whenever we read blind people's memoirs and biographies, we don't know how much each blind writer has internalized the sighted version of their lives, and thus perpetuate and 'sell' themselves as different and 'special'. It is the gap of not seeing that is the very thing that makes one different and, to be blunt, sells. The audience was warm and receptive, but I don't know how much I challenged their fixed notions of what blindness or blind dreams are.

By the time I got home, I found myself, as a modern woman learning to be blind, asking why it was not possible for blind people to have their own voice, unadulterated by layers of what is expected of them? If they try, like Helen Keller, are they ignored by sighted people? Must all blind people, and our sighted friends, perpetuate the often-stigmatizing tropes of talent, skill and inspiration? Are we all perpetuating the same erroneous myths?

Above all, by simply by writing this book, am I perpetuating more chirpy blind myths? And is it the reason, dear reader, you bought it?

*　　*　　*

What I sensed from all the nineteenth- and early twentieth-century narratives, some more benign than others, is how all these stories helped writers and readers, sighted or blind, to internalize a concept of blindness that has not changed much in the past thousand years. Even the most educated and financially supported blind people, such as Helen Keller, have been forced to fit into the boxes that sighted people understand. Such ideas serve to socially isolate blind people, and it is a view most blind people, me included, are deeply uncomfortable with today. The stories remind us that blindness, and the possibility of regaining sight, is at the heart of understanding punishment and redemption. As much as I admire Helen Keller, and other blind writers and poets such as Abram V. Courtney, Tilly Aston and the Argentinian poet Jorge Luis Borges, I have rarely found a blind writer or poet whom I chime with.

Can any narratives about blind people be trusted? Of late, there has been a glut of autobiographies from blind stars, including Trischa Zorn, the Paralympic swimmer; Sabriye Tenberken, who invented a new system of Braille for her fellow Tibetans; and the extraordinary human rights lawyer Haben Girma, who has been fighting for the rights of disabled people across the United States for the past two decades. As I read them, and even enjoy them, I have wondered: are drawn into such books by pity or voyeurism? Inspiration, even? Do sighted people fear that, if we are blind, we would feel completely at a loss? Perhaps.

But perhaps also most blind character stories (fictional or otherwise) are obliged to perpetuate the distinction between a blind and sighted world, rather than helping to bring the sighted and 'the blind' worlds together, because humans like binary opposites and easy labels. As the social historian Edward Said showed in *Orientalism* how Asian communities sold back to the colonies the exact image the imperialists wanted to see – people who were exotic, mysterious and obedient – so too Helen Keller and others have been obliged to fulfil sighted notions of blindness.

I suspect we are still doing it today – myself included.

7

Inventing it

The advantages of blindness (and disadvantages of tech)

I did not expect it, but when it came, I found myself lost for words.

This was the moment when my eye specialist finally told me that I was now, officially, 'legally blind'. He laid his hand on my arm in calm assurance when I looked alarmed and told me not to worry. It was simply a form that would mean I could ask for assistance from my council and 'prove' I was blind when I needed to. Given the bizarre number of people who had accused me of faking, like the mean train guard at King's Cross, it seemed a good idea.

He filled in a form and sent it off to the relevant department. I admit the idea of myself as 'legally' blind seemed both awful and hilarious. Did this mean that up to this point I had been 'illegally' blind? Had I been a renegade blind woman committing blind crimes for years? Could I have been arrested? I found myself wondering whether it was better than being legally bland or legally blonde. Above all, could I accept the word 'blind' to describe myself, given I could still see things – just? The specialist gave me a copy of the form and sent me home. Perhaps in denial, I forgot all about it.

Never underestimate the insistence of bureaucracy. Six weeks later, an enormous cylinder arrived, the kind that architects use for rolled-up blueprints. Inside, however, were schemes of a different sort. Just the physical act of reading the massive missive was absurd; it felt like the council had sent over the town crier, or at least its written equivalent. The 25 x 3-inch scroll, impressively festooned with formal and authoritative-looking stamps, informed me in 24-point font that my paperwork had been received, and I was now officially and certifiably 'legally blind'. I put the tube of doom in the drawer of many things and smirked at my new official label. To me there seemed an irony in that the very piece of paper that officially told me I couldn't see was itself hard to see. Then I went back to work.

A few months later, I received a call from the council's 'Mobility Team' who offered, at a slow pace, to send over a social worker to give me lessons on how to use a white cane, and how I could improve access to my home with some nifty tricks and adaptations. Another few months passed. Then, one day, a woman called Anna rang and asked, in a high-pitched squeaky voice that didn't endear her to me, if she could come over and meet me. We agreed a time and I braced myself for the visit, reminding myself not to be flippant, as is my wont.

Anna came with a huge heart and a huge backpack, which she plonked on the kitchen floor. She was deeply kind and enthusiastic: 'Oh how wonderfully you cook!' she cooed, when I showed her my risotto dish. 'And you find the bathroom and toilet routine easy?' Yes. (I wanted to be flippant: 'My tango is tricky because of the space, but generally it's fine.' I managed to keep quiet.) 'Fantastic', she said.

We sat down at the kitchen table, and I poured coffee. 'Oh!' she said enthusiastically, 'I have a great gadget for that', and whipped out a weirdly shaped bit of plastic with two metal prongs, which she hung over the mug. As I poured, little beeps sounded in the air, and thus told me when the mug was full. I squeaked back enthusiastically. She then pulled out other 'nifty things': a short white cane (a sight stick), wraparound dark glasses, two different cards with 'Taxi' and 'Bus' written on them to wave excitedly at anything that moved. It was rather like Christmas, but with a determinedly eager Santa. She was a treasure. 'Now I know these glasses are not very fashionable to young folks like you but try them – they really help block the glare.'

After showing me her amazing collection of nifty items, Anna stood up and offered to do some 'cane training' with me. There are a variety of white canes available, she told me – symbol canes, guide canes, and long canes – which all have their uses both to the blind person and the sighted world around you. There are also different ends to canes: pencil tips (for light contact with Mother Earth), marshmallow tips (a sort of golf ball shape, so you can feel the texture of the ground) and even a 'roller marshmallow tip', which allows you to roll your cane, as opposed to tapping the pavement. It was a whole new vocabulary and experience of the world, and part of me did not want to engage. That would mean I was more blind than sighted – a hard reality to accept.

My new friend pulled out something from her bag of tricks and declared: 'Today we are going to practise with a long cane.' She placed a folded oblong structure in my hands. I felt its smoothness and length, and as I removed the elastic rope from the top end, it snapped open in a magical springing motion. We stood up, and she stood beside me, asking me to bend my elbow at a right angle. 'Good!' she said. 'Now hold this cane so I can see if we have the right height cane – I have quite a few here.' She placed the cane firmly in my hand and guided me. 'Now put your thumb and finger here ... excellent ... and now see how it feels?' I nodded, and she put my thumb on the flat of the handle. It felt alien, as if holding a golf club for the first time (I am told). I moved around and danced, pretending to be a tap dancer.

Anna sighed at my flippancy and then took command. 'Okay, Selina, let's get this cane on the ground. It's your contact with the world. Let's use it!' I stopped being silly, and concentrated. 'The aim is to keep yourself in contact with reliable spaces and objects so you can position yourself in your environment. It's not perfect or always accurate, but it will give you a sense of your space, and when you might fall.' We ventured outside. There were three steps from my door, and she gave me clear instructions. 'Now use the cane to find the steps before you fall down them.' The cane went before me, tap tap tap, and felt ridiculous. She was very enthusiastic. 'Now remember, never touch the smelly end [the tip of the cane] as you don't know where it's been.' I noted this firmly in my head.

We moved onto the pavement. 'Good, take the cane in your right hand, good ... feel the weight? Great! Now sweep in an arc ... great.' This was all fine until she suggested I sweep left to my 'inner shore' and then right to my 'outer shore'. Then she pealed with laughter and said: 'Oh, I do get my right and left confused. I mean the other way. Ha ha!' I felt most unsure of my shores, but off we trundled.

Despite Anna's left-and-right challenges, we gently walked around the local square and learnt how to navigate pavements, stairs and traffic lights. My head held high and not looking at the ground, my feet did a great deal of navigating, and I felt like I was walking along a rickety bridge, hoping each slat would not give way. I learnt to navigate lampposts and trees, and Anna's stream of consciousness accompanied our walk. I spent a great deal of time concentrating on the sweep of my cane. When she delivered me back to my door, I sat in my kitchen alone and exhausted, contemplating the morning. Who was this woman I was becoming, bandying about with a cane and being cautious? Anna came regularly to visit me, and thanks to her and her colleague Paul, I have acclimatized to my cane; I have learnt to sashay, feeling the reach and sweep of my cane quite elegantly now. I can even whack annoying children and scooter riders on the pavement and look quite innocent as they moan from interrupting their gliding.

Learning practical things to help me navigate the world has been useful, but I also realize I am now beginning to wear the uniform of blindness. Not only have I learned to use a white cane and wear wraparound sunglasses when the light is too glaring, but I am also beginning to own my own sense of blindness. I have finally begun to accept I am 'severely sight impaired'. I find it easier to ask for help crossing roads, finding bus stops, stopping buses and negotiating uneven landscapes. I even ask to be shown where the toilet is (sigh).

I have also become accustomed to the various breaths of pity or fear when the white stick approaches, with me toddling behind. Sometimes I left the cane behind, just to have a day off from the reactions, but the falling over and bashing into lampposts was not always worth it. Somehow, and despite the bad days, I found myself more at ease with the myths the word and metaphor blindness holds, and the sound and rhythm of my cane. I accept I am still viewed by many as a *special person* who either needs pity or inspires inspiration. I have also learnt to accept (slowly) how blindness has changed the course of my daily life, internally and externally, as I have had to find a different path and avoid obstacles, whether physical or mental.

As I continue to work as a journalist and a disability advocate, the feeling of exhaustion and alienation does come and go and gets me frustrated, and my good friends are the only ones who see a glimpse of how much time I need to recover after a day out or travelling. New roads, new rooms, new tables and chairs – navigation needs a great deal of concentration. Fear needs a great deal of thought to be calmed. (Will I fall off the train track? Probably not. Will I be judged for being blind at a job interview? Probably.) Explaining to people, yet again, that I cannot be fixed, that guide dogs are not a solution for everyone, and white canes can only take you so far, takes graciousness – and for those I lose my temper with, apologies: I sometimes don't have the strength to be polite.

* * *

It seems many people have struggled with sight loss as I have. But also the past reveals there are many blind men and women who have invented tools, objects and techniques which have given them the freedom to move and live independently over the centuries.

Take the history of raised letters, whether via some form of raised wood, stone, or leather letters. I had no idea that archaeologists have found evidence to show that blind people have read letters and created blocks to write with as early as the fourth century AD, albeit with some money and friends to help. We know from detailed notes, for example, that the scholar Didymus read by using carved wooden letters. A thousand years later, Geronimo Cardano, the Italian physician, philosopher and mathematician, advocated the use of touch for blind people on raised wooden blocks. In the sixteenth century, Francesco Lucas of Saragossa, Spain, also incised letters on thin wooden tablets. A few more inventions emerged in the seventeenth century, with a German doctor creating wax-covered tablets that blind people could write on.

Over in France, a few experimented with creating blocks of embossed wood or leather with movable lead letters. Most of these cumbersome systems remained in the hands of those who could afford them, and the luxury of an amanuensis. Even for these lucky few, there was a very limited selection of reading material available, usually religious.

As the nineteenth century rolled in, however, a few pioneers, both blind and sighted, longed to bring blind people to the new trend of education and philanthropy. They argued that reading was an essential part of a blind person's education, and there was a push to create systems of reading which were also reliant on touching embossed letters and figures. At the school for blind youth in Paris, for example, students were taught to slowly trace their fingers over raised Roman alphabet text and work out sentences word by word. This system was slow and cumbersome. The inventor, Valentin Haüy (the director of the school), found working with his blind students very helpful, as they showed him what worked for them, rather than assuming what worked with their sighted teachers. In line with this, he designed and manufactured books which, while expensive and complicated to create (Haüy's school only had three of these types of books when it opened), represented one of the first systems to rely on touch to read, showing that reading methods had an alternative.

It is no surprise that some sighted educators questioned whether a universal reading system would benefit blind people at all. The moment Haüy opened his doors to blind students in Paris in 1784, for example, discussions ensued over whether blind people *should* be included or excluded in the world of books and writing. If so, should a special system be created, or should a system close to the sighted world's books be relied on? For some, there was a deep-seated fear that learning to read would distract students from remunerative labour.

At the same time, there was also the question of how blind people should play a part in the world they would choose to read. Indeed, before the concept of raised print, blind students had little option to read other than to memorize by rote. Institutions insisted on their students being given only practical information and basic religious grounding. In 1833, one school reported that the inmates had 'voluntarily committed to memory the whole of the psalms contained in the book of common prayer. This they have done in a shorter length of time than has been done in any similar institution.' Religion seemed to offer the most palatable books of choice, whether blind people liked it or not.

The good news was that it was a blind student of Haüy's who became the instigator of creating an alternative system of reading for blind people. Frustrated with the limited amount of reading he could achieve alone, according to the almost mythic story told to all French school children, the young Louis Braille strove to find a reading system for blind people that bridged the gap between the sighted and blind worlds. Having tried a system called 'night writing', a military coded embossed script invented by Charles Barbier to pass military notes down the line during battle, Louis decided to simplify the reading process by creating at first a twelve, but ultimately a six-dot matrix or 'cell' system, where each dotted formation on the matrix represented a letter. The aim was to make each cell recognizable with one touch of the finger.

At first, Louis created sixty-three combinations of the six dots to represent the letters of the alphabet and certain common words and numbers. The model was later extended to include musical notation. In 1829, he launched his system in a book entitled *Method of Writing Words, Music and Plain Songs by Means of Dots, for Use by the Blind and Arranged for Them*. Braille revised and republished the book in 1837 to include methods for writing algebra and arithmetic. Blind students loved the ease and fluidity of being able to read and write with the system, though sighted professors were not so keen.

Other blind schools also tended towards raised touch systems but, turning away from Braille, raised Roman letters also emerged. Many sighted directors believed the advantages of both teacher and student reading the same letters outweighed the expense of such enterprises, and they rejected Braille on the basis that it was a completely different system from the Roman alphabet. There was also the issue that sighted tutors could not see or understand it.

Other sighted inventors also thought they knew better than their blind students. The School for the Blind in Edinburgh, for example, backed and used an embossed alphabet by a printer called James Gall with some success. Gall devised a relief alphabet which echoed the conventional Roman alphabet but replaced the curved letters with angular shapes. The Edinburgh asylum tried and endorsed it, as did the Glasgow Asylum for the Blind, which in turn asked for it to be sanctioned by the Royal Society in Edinburgh. In the same way that Haüy won approval of his school from the most illustrious intellectual institutions of Paris, so too did Gall win the backing of Edinburgh's intellectual elite. He even advertised his Roman alphabet system in local newspapers, calling for a public subscription and other philanthropic institutions to raise funds to take his alphabet further. But it took until 1832 to get enough funding to put together his first complete book, *The Gospel of St John*. He modified the design over the years, and even issued an entire New Testament, embossed music and relief maps. But his output was too small, and he did not manage to find any major financial backing.

Down on the south coast in Brighton, Dr William Moon was also devising his own reading system. Dr Moon, who lost his sight when he was twenty-one, created his own alphabet that he wanted to be 'open and clear to the touch'. Originally published in 1845, and later in his book *Light for the Blind* in 1877, Moon's reading system quietly echoed the Roman alphabet, made from large curves, angles and lines. Its advantages were many compared to Braille: it was translatable to other languages and its shapes were similar to Roman letters, which helped those who lost their sight later on in life. Missionaries in Africa and China relied heavily on Moon type as it was easy for the sighted to translate. There were also reading systems invented by Edmund Fry and Francesco Lucas.

What was clear to many blind people in the nineteenth century was that there was not one homogeneous class of blind people and readers, and for each reading system endorsed, there were critics for and against it. By 1852, for example, the Edinburgh Asylum stocked at least four different systems of reading material: by Moon, Lucas, Braille and Fry. Blind people themselves argued that different ages and intelligence required different systems, not one universal system. As became increasingly evident, as displayed at the Great Exhibitions of 1850 and 1862, there were a variety of methods offered. By the middle of the century, it was decided by the great and good – and sighted – that embossed reading should be in Roman alphabet, and this decision was ratified by the grand jury at the 1851 Great Exhibition at Crystal Palace. The judges argued that 'the adoption of any arbitrary system will do much to cut them off still more from communion with their fellow man'.[1]

In some ways I can understand why the Roman system won favour with the sighted community; it is a recognizable alphabet that has been used globally for centuries. By the mid-nineteenth century, US institutions also seemed to be heading that way, with Gridley Howe, the director of the Perkins Institute for the Blind in Boston (where Helen Keller was studying), inventing his own Roman embossed system. The Roman alphabet was reliable because it also

---

[1] Phillips, *The Blind in British Society*, p. 44.

allowed blind people to master any type of literature, despite being awkward and large to create.

At the first conference in Europe of teachers of the blind in 1873, Thomas Rhodes Armitage, a blind leader of an English charity (now RNIB), argued that Braille was the choice of many blind students. In 1882, Armitage reported: 'There is now probably no institution in the civilized world where Braille is not used except in some in North America.'[2] Braille was officially adopted by schools for the blind in the United States in 1916 and formalized as a universally used system in 1932, just over a hundred years after a blind man had invented it. It is still very much in use today across the world, in many languages, although with the arrival of audio technology, its use is in decline.

Inventions, however bumpy, can be great things. I have many blind friends who tell me their lives would never be as enriched and fulfilled if they had not had a life of private Braille reading. As I have said above, having someone read to you is lovely – either live or through an audio book – but being able to read words directly and imagine how Lady Macbeth feels when washing her hands after murdering someone is fantastic.

---

[2]Phillips, *The Blind in British Society*.

Not all reading inventions work for everyone. For a start, not all blindness is the same, and learning Braille later in life can be a big challenge, especially for people with diabetes as they often lose the sense of touch in their fingers. For many, young or old, Braille can be like learning a new language, which some people have a talent for and others don't. Two years into my training, and quietly enjoying lying in the dark and reading at bedtime, it is still hard for me to read fluently, and I often revert to audio books simply because I am tired of concentrating so hard to read the raised dots.

It was surprising to find, too, there is a debate about the future of Braille. Its use is in decline, and as it is replaced by voiceovers and audio tech solutions, there is a question about whether or not Braille is still useful in the twenty-first century. For myself and my blind friends, any device that allows blind people to have access to the printed word is important. As Sandy Murillo, a writer in San Francisco, recently argued so eloquently, 'Nothing can substitute the sense of independence, and thus confidence, in reading and choosing what to read, for oneself'.[3]

* * *

---

[3] Sandy Murillo works at The Chicago Lighthouse, an organization serving the blind and visually impaired. https://chicagolighthouse.org/sandys-view/commentary-is-braille-still-important/

Other inventions have also changed the life of blind people, and none so much as the training of guide dogs. Possibly because of our love of canines and the sense they are man's best friend, the amount of support sighted folk give guide dog charities is astounding. The well-loved British children's programme *Blue Peter* raised millions of pounds over the years for guide dogs,[4] and often gave their Golden Retriever litter to such charities to train them as guide dogs.

Canine friends have existed for centuries. While the domestication of dogs probably happened around 150,000 years ago, there is no real evidence of dogs leading blind people until around 1 AD, where a few ancient murals in the ruins of Herculaneum, just outside Rome, show blind men being led by dogs. A scroll found in China, now in the Metropolitan Museum in New York, dated from around 1200 AD, shows a blind man (his eyes covered) being led by a dog. Other records from Asia and Europe up to the Middle Ages also show dogs leading blind men.

The first systematic attempt to train dogs to aid blind people, however, occurred around 1780 at Les Quinze-Vingts hospital for the blind in Paris. I say attempt, because we don't have much information, and I somehow imagine

---

[4]https://www.sightsavers.org/news/2018/10/60-years-of-blue-peter/

that for thousands of years dogs were devoted companions to their blind owners and knew their way home. But in terms of formal training, we know that in 1788 a blind sieve maker from Vienna trained a Spitz to guide him so well that people often questioned whether he was blind. In 1819, Dr Johann Wilhelm Klein, founder of the Institute for the Education of the Blind (*Blinden-Erziehungs-Institut*) in Vienna, mentioned the concept of the guide dog in his book on educating blind people and described his method for training dogs. A Swiss man, Jakob Birrer, wrote in 1847 about his experiences of being guided over a period of five years by a dog he had specially trained.

The more modern guide dog story, along with the harnesses and clever beasts stopping at traffic lights, came from the trained dogs used in the First World War, and the thousands of soldiers returning from the front blinded, often by poison gas. A German doctor, Dr Gerhard Stalling, got the idea when, walking with a patient one day through the hospital grounds, he was called away and left his dog with the patient as company. When he returned, he saw signs, from the way the dog was behaving, that it was guarding, and even guiding, the blind patient towards him. Dr Stalling started, with his patients, to explore ways of training dogs to become reliable guides, and in August 1916 opened the world's first guide dog school for the blind in Oldenburg. The school grew and many new branches opened across Germany, training up to 600 dogs a year.

These schools provided dogs not only to ex-servicemen, but also to blind people in Britain, France, Spain, Italy, the United States, Canada and the then Soviet Union. Owing to lack of funds and suitable canines, the venture had to shut down in 1926. But another large guide dog training centre opened near Berlin, which broke new ground in the training of guide dogs; it was capable of accommodating around 100 dogs at a time and providing up to twelve fully trained guide dogs a month.

The guide dog-fest really got going when a wealthy American woman, Dorothy Harrison Eustis, who was already training dogs for the army, police and customs service in Switzerland, heard about other dog training for blind people. Miss Dorothy was curious to study the Berlin school's methods and spent several months there. She came away so impressed that she wrote an article about it for the *Saturday Evening Post* in the United States in October 1927. A blind American man, Morris Frank, heard about the article and bought a copy of the newspaper. He later said that the five cents the newspaper cost him 'bought an article that was worth more than a million dollars to me. It changed my life.' He wrote to Eustis, telling her that he would very much like to help introduce guide dogs to the United States.

Taking up the challenge, Eustis trained a dog, Buddy, and brought Frank over to Switzerland to learn how to work with the dog. Frank went back to the United States with what many believe to be the country's first guide dog. Meanwhile, an Italian guide dog organization, *Sculola Nazionale Cani Guida per Ciechi*, was also established in 1928. The success of the United States experience encouraged Eustis to set up a guide dog school at Vevey in Switzerland in 1928. She called this school, like the one a year later in New Jersey, 'L'Oeil qui voit', or 'The Seeing Eye' (the name comes from the Old Testament of the Bible – 'the hearing ear and the seeing eye'; Proverbs 20.12).

The schools in Vevey, New Jersey and Italy were the first guide dog schools of the modern era that have survived the test of time. In 1931, the first four British guide dogs completed their training, and three years later the Guide Dogs for the Blind Association was founded in the UK. Since then, guide dog schools have opened all round the world, and more open their doors every decade.

It goes without saying that thousands of people have had their lives transformed by guide dogs, thanks to the organizations that provide them. The commitment of the people who work for these organizations, and the people who financially support them, is as strong today as it ever was, and the heirs of Dorothy Eustis's legacy continue to work for the increased mobility, dignity and independence of blind and partially sighted people the world over. The movement goes on.

*   *   *

I am often asked: why don't I have a guide dog? And of course, I understand that implicit in this question is: why wouldn't every blind person want a boon companion? To be honest, I really don't want to deal with so much, including the dog poo – finding it, picking it up and then carrying it around till I find a bin. I think I would have a problem with that even if sighted.

You may smile at this, but I can only tell you that I am not good with the entire dog story. Last year, while tending to my mother, who was not well and has two lovely dogs, I began smelling a terrible odour around the house, and decided to investigate. After ten minutes, I called my sister in the United States, and we spent two hours (two whole hours!) using the camera on my mobile phone looking for dog poo. It was awful. I waved my phone over various floors and my sister had to yell 'Stop! Back a bit. Nope! It's a leaf' or 'Nope! That's your shoe!' I waved the phone backwards and forwards until, finally, the afternoon ended with me stepping in the offending object in the front hall while going backwards from a camera sweep. It squished underfoot and gave way all across the carpet. The dogs wagged their tails with delight and then walked the poo all over the house. I was grateful it was my sister on the phone, not my helpful social worker. I am sure fully trained guide dogs would never do such things, but it did put me off my dinner for some time.

But I am also cautious regarding the current rules as to who decides to grant one a guide dog. At an interview with Guide Dogs five years ago, I remember that three people – all sighted, and not trained medical professionals – asked me about lack of sight and my life as a working woman, to see if I could manage a guide dog. It was incredibly intrusive and almost insulting, and I found myself excluded from the discussion to decide if having a dog was right for me. The questions they asked me suggested that the guide dog had more rights than I did as a blind person, and somehow it did not feel right. I believe that the various interviews have changed since then.

Moreover, if you have a guide dog in the UK or the United States, the society for guide dogs owns them and can take away the animal at any time if they believe you are not worthy or treating your dog appropriately. Such a caveat might make sense – especially if your blind buddy mistreats you. But who decides if you are worthy enough and doing a good job as a blind person? While you might berate me for moaning, consider whether you would want your life decided for you, simply because you had one leg.

There is also a whiff of 'miracle working' with a guide dog – as if the blind person who relies on the dog is somehow not important and the dog is. A friend who has a guide dog says he is constantly shocked how everyone talks to the guide dog, and not the person behind the dog.

While the concept of a guide dog is lovely, and has helped many millions of people find an independence they presumed they had lost, I also know many blind friends who agree with me: guide dogs are not for everyone.

* * *

You will be pleased to hear that my scepticism does have a day off. Every now and then, I have a sense of knowing the world differently from the sighted world and feeling slightly smug that I am enjoying private and interesting things that the sighted world does not. As the writer Thomas Blacklock said in 1776, there are *advantages* to blindness, and there have been for centuries.

My favourite advantage is the wonderful world of audio description, or AD, as it's commonly known. For those who don't know, AD is a verbal commentary providing visual information for those unable to perceive it themselves. Usually heard via a headset, AD is a narration that helps you 'see' when you are watching theatre, films, sports and other cultural events. Over the past few years, I have seen quite a few shows that have AD performance, and it has given me access to precise facial cues that I, as someone with little sight, would never see. At *Amadeus* at the National Theatre, I was informed through my earpiece that 'She [Mozart's wife] looks at the palms of her hands sadly, and softly turns away'. I was also told about the physicality of the orchestra, which was an integral part of the action on stage.

If you like ballet and dancing, which I sometimes do, AD can really change the game. Watching and listening to Steven Spielberg's AD of *West Side Story*, having someone describing how a dancer moves – swivel, turn, bend, tap – really does give you the sense of how a body works when dancing and how it interacts with others.

Of course, as with any modern inventions, you must be careful with whom you choose to watch and listen to AD. My sister and I went to see the first *Fifty Shades of Grey* film a few years back, and even though we both knew the film was going to be cheesy, and, well, pornographic, I convulsed so hard with laughter I snorted cola out of my nose. I tried to control myself, but when I heard phrases such as 'Christian pulls down her underwear. He spanks her bottom. He spanks her again. She smiles', I fell off the velvet cushioned seat and onto the popcorn-covered floor. The sibling was mortified. Afterwards, I had to explain that hearing American accents having rampant sex – 'Anastasia!' 'Christian!' – while a rather bored English voice describes the scene with the enthusiasm of someone reading their tax return was comedic genius.

When I am not reviewing bad porn, my favourite shows are the descriptions on Scandi dramas and crime thrillers. They are so detailed and rhythmic – akin to an afternoon play on the radio. 'He raises the knife – he plunges it down, again and again and again. She slides down against the kitchen cupboard – blood pours out of her mouth and into a pool to the floor.' *Silent Witness* (and my ironing) on a Monday evening has never been so riveting.

But while having a voice in your ear giving you audio descriptions or even audio directions is liberating, it also means you are concentrating very hard on the voice in your earpiece. I am often exhausted from following the language in my earpiece and balancing with the minute bits I can see on stage. Even if I shut my eyes, sometimes I am late to the party. When the audience is laughing raucously, my audio describer is a minute behind. As I explain to my friends, I often have no idea why everyone is laughing.

While having Benedict Cumberbatch read your directions to Manchester is sublime, at some point you just need to get there. For me, and other blind friends, there is something calming about the ability to digest the instructions in your own mind – not through another's voice (however sexy).

*   *   *

But this is not the place to moan. Audio description is amazing, and I heartily urge everyone to use it, blind or not. Inventions such as AD are exciting and have become one of many modern supports that make the blind life more manageable and accessible.

But what I often find hard to explain to people is that inventions, tech and new gadgets don't necessarily stop the experience of sight loss, and always take a great deal of learning. Inventions to help blind people have been created in many different guises and moments, so I suspect the cane and sunglasses will be very much out of date in a hundred years' time, and we will all be walking around with implants and lenses with microchips in them. But it's not always a solution.

Take the wonderful world of applications – or apps – for example. It excites sighted people a great deal that there are apps that read your messages and emails for you, take dictation, and even guide you via a map. All are very helpful in many ways, as is a cane, a guide dog, or even raised dots to read books. All seem to offer freedom to the oft-imagined, dreadful plight of a blind person. I cannot count the times sighted people tell me the wonder of smartphones and how my life must have changed because of these ingenious devices.

And it is true that my independence has been immensely helped by my phone. But just think about it: sliding your finger around a smooth screen with no ridges or bumps to guide you, in the hope you will find the right app, is quite a skill. It takes time and training. It's also exhausting.

Then there is the 'speech-to-text' technology, which is quite amazing, and which I have used a great deal to write this book. There are well-meaning sighted folk who gasp at how well you read your email, your messages, take notes, even offer sight via your camera. They coo with excitement: 'Have you seen that new app, Be My Eyes? You just dial in, and someone in the world will read whatever you need!' I find myself enthusing as well: 'Yesss!' I can then tell the story of how, when stuck on a train station in Berlin, I could not find a platform number and used the aforementioned app. A voice twanged a lovely greeting: 'Hi! I am Amy! How can I help you?' I explained the problem. 'Oh honey,' she said, 'I can't help you! I don't read German!' and hung up. I did not have time to explain that numbers are numbers, even in Germany. I rang my sister at 6 a.m. in Iowa and woke her eyes up instead. I am not being ungrateful. I am just pointing out that the magic of an app and connecting you to a random stranger doesn't always work. There is a fantasy of self-reliance, but as it turns out, things, eyes, and even dogs and people can fail.

Beware also of talking to nerds and geeks who tell you of sci-fi inventions and hopes, such as self-driving cars, implants, cyborgs, and the joys of artificial intelligence.[5] I may regret writing this and be zooming around ten years hence, being supremely excited about going somewhere on my own, but I am not sure. The idea of being reliant on a large lump of metal run by a computer, with no ability to stop, swerve or even avoid objects, sends chills down my spine and white cane. Yet I am frequently told how amazing my life will be because soon I could have a cyborg helper, or a chip that will see for me. Indeed, I will not 'need' anyone. Somehow the 'fix' of technology means the able-bodied and, in my case, sighted people in the world will feel less, well, anxious and guilty about my allegedly tragic and impossible life.

I also want to ask: do any of us want to have a chip inserted in our arms that could guide us, but was owned by a corporation that at any point could take the chip out, or amend it, without consent? Would you want a corporation to make billions from a blind-supporting program or

---

[5] https://mobilesyrup.com/2021/12/09/blind-canadian-jaclyn-pope-esight-4-accessible-apps/?fbclid=IwAR1Tt8lIufbfNhpiw7aD_pwlKiv9zmvoWvwe9QCOiOyyojXrpvlWdxvdPH

software that only lets you have access to their technology for a price?

In answer to the last question, this is already happening. There are programs that my special blind technology cannot read. I can get access to a text-reading app, but only for an annual fee of over £750 plus tax. I worry blind and other disabled people are being left behind in the technological revolution. So while inventions, dogs, adaptions and apps are truly ingenious, perhaps it is right and proper we question their role in our lives and who decides what, when and how we have access to them. As I said at the start of this chapter, not all inventions are for everyone, and we should not presume otherwise ...

* * *

To be clear, I am not rejecting any of these remarkable inventions. Because of my mobile phone, my cane, and audio description, I certainly have found most allow an easier life – and often a great deal of fun.

But I would also argue gently that they also come with a health warning. It turns out computers, cars, mobiles and humans can fail, and don't fix society. In the same way, inventions are like miracle cures. There is often an implicit suggestion that if a blind person has the apps, the dog, the tech, they will not be tragic or a burden. I am not the first with such thoughts. A friend who is a wheelchair user says people endlessly tell her about new back implants, or new robot wheelchairs that can climb stairs. She says that is great and dandy, but why not build a ramp in the first place that everyone, including mothers with pushchairs or people with heavy shopping, can use?

As I found when exploring blindness medicine and fixing, there is an inherent desire to cure disease and impairment, often without the consent of the subject. Perhaps it is primal; to see anyone in our tribe suffering (even presumed) triggers all sorts of anxieties about feeding, hunting, procreating and protecting ourselves. So away from blame, what would make our presumed terrible blind lives easier, more fluid, without inflicting the rule of sight on a blind person?

For most blind people, the answer is simple. Absolutely *do* invent. *Do* create solutions to any problem and disability. But just ask and include us on the journey first. Find out what we want, rather than presuming what our needs are. I understand your goodwill and good intentions, but like you, I want the ability to choose.

Above all, don't assume we live in a world that does not believe our lives are tragic or heroic. We all just want to live our lives as we see fit. Try to see the world through our eyes – blind or not.

Conclusion

What is blindness anyway?

I have no problem standing up and screaming, 'hey, let's go, come on, let's make a change'... And I'm just looking for people to back me behind that so that I don't think I'm crazy. Because when I'm told to sit on the couch and sit in the dark, be quiet, be complacent and sit on the shelf and do nothing, that's when there's something wrong. That's when we should all be standing up.

JACLYN POPE, MOBILESYRUP, 9 DECEMBER 2021[1]

So what has Nandy, the blind Neanderthal who we met at the start of the journey, taught me?

The answer is many things all at the same time. On the one hand, I am sitting in my study at the end of 2022, using my very clever speech-to-text technology to finish this book, and thinking about my past week, past year and past decade. Part of me would like to show how I come to

---

[1] Pope, Jaclyn. 'Why Assistive Technology Matters to Me: Jaclyn Pope – AdaptiVision' (lowvisionsource.com).

terms with my blindness, and how sighted people consider blindness.

I also wish to show how this search through history – classical, biblical, medieval and Enlightenment periods, not to mention the nineteenth and twentieth centuries – has shown me how blind people have always been considered part of humanity as each age requires, and while the past was not so pleasant, thank goodness we are all so modern and decent now. I would love to write how sometimes the perception of blindness was good and useful, sometimes bad and evil, and each sighted generation used the notion of not seeing as a way of differentiating and distancing themselves from blind people, but now, in the modern world, we are so much better than this.

But sadly, it's still difficult. Just last week, I was filming a news piece about a new app for blind people, and the cameraman came up to me and said in a very kind voice: 'Could you act more blind, my lovely?' I replied: 'What do you mean?' He said: 'Well, you know, stretch your arms out a bit, sort of fumble for the door. Show us you can't find it . . .' I said: 'Er, I don't think blind people behave like that. A door is not so hard to find really.' He seemed disappointed.

On the same day, I caught the train back home to London. As I scrolled through Twitter, as I do when sitting on trains, I found the following tweets, which reminded me yet again how being blind in the twenty-first century is complicated. A variety of blind people are now taking to social media to document how they are treated. One tweet read: 'My best attempts to explain why it's a bad idea to grab hold of blind people without knowledge or consent.'[2] Another read: '"You cope really well" is often the compliment I get at the gym!! "Goodness aren't you determined." Trying not to respond these days is hard.'[3] Finally, a passenger wrote: 'I've been refused the PRM assistance I booked @BritishAirways unless I sit in a wheelchair. I am blind, not a wheelchair user. This is totally unacceptable.'[4] I know what they mean.

It would be nice to smile, nod and say yes, such tweets show us that things happen, but in general life is better, and how helpful it is to hear such stories in the public domain. In quiet moments, I also know that I have found unexpected stories of talented and ordinary blind folk – superheroes and supposed burdens – and understood how art and fiction perpetuated our notions of a supposedly static, burdensome and innocent blind person. I really want to write that I am happy how the worlds of dogs, canes, tech and invention have been game changers for blind people. Fallible they may be, but wow, how they help us lead independent lives.

---

[2] Sean Dilley NEWS – twitter 8.03pm 8 December 2022.
[3] DaftApteh @madanna69 – twitter 3.21pm 19 November 2022.
[4] Sean Dilley NEWS – twitter 9.30am 20 November 2022.

Yet what I have really learnt from this book is how few voices of actual blind people are available to us, even now. This is because blindness has always been considered a separate and dangerous state simply because sighted people don't understand that it is neither other nor alien.

I have grasped, too, despite the plethora of memoir and super-crip worshipping, the happy ending narratives about blind people are unrealistic and misleading. Mostly this is because none of us can always be perky and positive, forgiving and gracious, or even calm and at peace with our lot all the time: I certainly can't. This is not because of my blindness. Mostly it's because I love life and am endlessly curious about how and why people do things, and because I am, as my husband will tell you, deeply impatient. There is never enough time, and I am always gadding about (and falling over), but always up to something.

A more accurate conclusion for me here might be that exploring the history of blindness has given me a different perspective, and I understand more about why people treat blind people differently. While Nandy the Neanderthal taught me to dig deep in the hidden caves by the Tigris River, he taught me too we need to bring more stories about blindness and disability to life and share them, so that we can all see ourselves in all our variants.

I also understand how none of us are allowed to indulge in any moral smugness. When I started this quest, I must confess I was as biased and ignorant as everyone else. I, like the rest of the seeing population, presumed blindness was total darkness – a tragedy, a burden, and a state to be feared. But because of my own current life experience, a great deal of time in libraries researching, and simply from talking to other blind people, I have come to understand being blind is so much more than not seeing. It is part of being human. No more, no less. I learnt that aligning oneself to the word 'blind' and 'blindness', whether completely blind or not, can be a useful signpost, but is usually complicated.

* * *

Has my notion of blindness changed, though?

Absolutely yes. Perhaps my most basic learning is that, whether from birth, accident, war or disease, it is a state of non-seeing, and that's all. It really is not a tragic, fixed state, or even a heroic one. It is not a negative or a catastrophic state, but the negative labels are misapplied because usually blindness occurs in dramatic or catastrophic circumstances. While technology and medical interventions have certainly changed and improved, our views and attitudes remain entrenched, naïve and patronizing.

You would be surprised by the number of people who tilt their heads sceptically when I claim there is no exact cure for my condition because it is too difficult to operate on. You would smile at the strangers who tell me that my hearing, sense of touch and smell must surely be miraculously compensated owing to my lack of sight. You will be shocked when I tell you the abuse I have experienced when walking out with my white cane. It still shocks me, and often reminds me how harsh the world can be. Writing this book has helped understand why people are cruel and mean; they know no better. But it doesn't stop the hurt and humiliation.

But I do ask myself: has researching this book taught me some good things too and that there are advantages to being blind?

Well, yes. Let us celebrate the technology and inventions that benefit us all, not just blind people. Let us sing the praises of audio description – you can drive and listen to a movie without watching a screen. Older friends love haptic technology, which buzzes and shakes their phones, so they can feel the ring if they are losing their hearing. Lovely, whether in our pockets or handbags.

And historical research? I can only yell: 'More please!' Now we have more of a roadmap, we have the ammunition to challenge misconceptions about blindness. Blindness shows that no human is perfect, and the 'imperfect' does not always have to be fixed. Blindness in all its forms is part of us all, and more than likely always will be. I feel that by investigating blindness history, and how we have all 'imagined' blindness, we can choose how blindness is seen.

Indeed, this word – 'imagine' – is the key to understanding why we are all fascinated and frightened of blindness; it is our own notions and traditions attached to the state of not seeing, layered and encrusted over time, which have shaped our notion of what blindness means, rather than an understanding of the actual, neutral, physical state of not seeing.

My hope is that this book has given a few more voices to the blind people unrecognized on the hillside of history. While many blind men have had biographies written about them, I hope there will be more examples to show that there are a good number of blind women who have had amazing, sometimes silent, careers and domestic lives. We need to hear more stories, whether from those who talk about how bereft of the world they feel because they cannot see, or from people who found new courage and new life in their sightlessness. There is no judgement either way. We need to hear *all* these voices – in all their diversity – so to manage our own experiences and expectations.

Finally, I hope this book has, in its own small way, broken down a few more of these myths and stereotypes, and helped to dispel them for all of us. I hope it helps us to see how our notions of blindness have changed over time and reflect how we all 'see' ourselves, blind or otherwise.

ACKNOWLEDGEMENTS

As most writers know, no book is possible without some phenomenal support.

Without doubt, the midwife extraordinaire was the novelist and mentor and kindest of friends, Mavis Cheek. In the dark days of lockdown, my email box was full of encouragement, humour and writing wisdom, and it is fair to say that Mavis stopped me wandering off like a Labrador into the woods, always with gentle good cheer. At the same time, thank you to the glorious Caroline Michel and her team at Peters Fraser and Dunlop. Caroline found the book a safe haven with Bloomsbury, and she and Kieron Fairweather fought my corner firmly with grace.

We were also lucky to find the professorial and kind David Avital as an editor at Bloomsbury Academic, who inherited me from the wonderful Iradj Bagherzade. We are all so sad Iradj is not here to see the finalized manuscript, but I treasure our lunches and phone chats over the years. We spoke a month before he died, and he knew the book was about to go into production. I hope I have done his belief in me justice.

Behind the scenes there are many amazing friends and colleagues who understood what a complicated subject blindness is. Professor Hannah Thompson embraced me into the world of academia, and consistently gave me wise and clever feedback. The community of thinkers, writers and academics who welcomed me to conferences, seminars, dinners and congresses around the subject of disability and blindness has been a lesson in inclusivity. Thank you, Georgina Kleege, Cathy Kudlick, Zina Weygand, Heather Tilley, Matt Rubury, Stephen Kuusisto, Kate Tunstall. Thanks to those no longer with us, Brian Miller and Jonathan Riley-Smith, who both gave me the keys to unlocking obscure and invisible histories.

Of great importance has been the backing of the writing community, including the Society of Authors, and the Royal Society of Literature who funded me when there were no funds. 'Women Who Write', who have met online, wherever we are in the world, every two to three weeks for the past few years made the writing journey far less lonely. Aside from being wonderful friends, they gave me often needed knowledge and clarity, not to mention warm moral support. Thank you, wise women: Carla Power, Anna Minton, Beth Gardner, Moni Moshin, Natasha Randall. Thanks always to Homa Rastegar Driver and Rosie and

ACKNOWLEDGEMENTS

Paul Bigmore who reminded me of the importance of family life.

Writing is a lonely task, so I must give a deep bow to my sister Kassia Scott, who was there from the very beginning. Her powers of research and endless enthusiasm never cease to amaze me. She drove me far and wide to research, often when she was busy teaching – and our conversations over education and parenting have given me deep insight into raising kids. My nephews, Callum and William Scott, have also been an endless source of invigoration as they have grown up, and have kept me up to date with superhero trends and youthful thinking.

Many people have helped me write and edit when my eyes were struggling, or my mood was sad and low. My thanks must go to the lovely Anna Landre, who typed while I talked out loud. Thanks too to close and steady friends such as Oliver Wells, Nadia Martini, Anne McCabe, Astrid Winkler-Studd (and family), Stefanie Oswalt (and family) and Foteini Georganta Romanov (and family) who never doubted me when I doubted myself and urged me to stay the course. And thanks to my mother. She will be relieved she does not have to ask me 'How's the book going?' without fearing groans of despondency.

The final word must go to my husband, Naci Mehmet. He is the wisest, honest, and most humorous fellow a girl could live with, and I would be lost without his minutia detector. Thank you, my dearest *herif*, for holding my hand, endless cups of tea, and for making sense of my confused thinking. Love as a word simply doesn't cover it.

London, July 2022

BIBLIOGRAPHY

Sources used for blindness data and definitions

Encyclopaedia Britannica. Entries on blind/blindness over time – 1775, 1828, 1850, 1870, 1900, 1914, 1917

Fight for Sight: http://www.fightforsight.org.uk/about-the-eye/facts-about-sight-loss/?gclid=CI3y8Y_b48sCFVQ_GwodTqEFVA

National Federation for the Blind (USA) Homepage. National Federation of the Blind (nfb.org)

Royal National Institute of Blind People (UK) Key information and statistics on sight loss in the UK. RNIB

World Health Organization: Blindness and vision impairment (who.int)

Disability, blindness and visual studies – general

Barasch, Moshe. *The History of a Mental Image in Western Thought: Blindness*. New York: Routledge, 2001.

Berger, John. *Ways of Seeing*. London: British Broadcasting Corporation and Penguin Books, 1972.

Bickel, Lennard. *Triumph Over Darkness: The Life of Louis Braille*. Sydney: Allen & Unwin Australia, 1998.

Bolt, David. *The Metanarrative of Blindness: A Re-Reading of Twentieth-Century Anglophone Writing*. University of Michigan Press, 2014.

Derrida, Jacques. *Memoirs of the Blind. The Self-Portrait and Other Ruins*. Trans. Pascale-Anne Brault and Michael Naas. University of Chicago Press, 1993.

Farrell, Gabriel. *The Story of Blindness*. Cambridge, MA: Harvard University Press, 1956.

Gregory, R. L. *Eye and Brain: The Psychology of Seeing*. 2nd edn. New York: McGraw-Hill, 1973.

Gigante, Denise. 'Facing the Ugly: The Case of Frankenstein'. *English Literary History* 67 (2000): 565–87.

Goffman, Erving. *Stigma – Notes on the Management of Spoiled Identity*. London: Penguin Books, 1963.

Hays, Peter L. *The Limping Hero: Grotesques in Literature*. New York University Press, 1971.

Holmes, Martha Stoddard. *Fictions of Affliction: Physical Disability in Victorian Culture*. Ann Arbor, MI: University of Michigan Press, 2004.

Jay, Martin. *Downcast Eyes: The Denigration of Vision in Twentieth-Century French Thought*. University of California Press, 1994.

Joshua, Essaka. '"Blind Vacancy": Sighted Culture and Voyeuristic Historiography in Mary Shelley's Frankenstein'. *European Romantic Review* 22(1) (2011): 46–69.

Kleege, Georgina. 'Blindness and Visual Culture: An Eye Witness Account', in Lennard J. Davis (ed.), *The Disability Studies Reader*. 2nd edn. New York and Oxford: Routledge, 2006, pp. 391–8.

Kleege, Georgina. *Sight Unseen*. London: Yale University Press, 1999.

Kudlick, J. Catherine. 'Disability History: Why We Need Another "Other"'. *American Historical Review* 108(3) (June 2003): 763–93.

Mitchell, David T., and Snyder, L. Sharon. *Narrative Prosthesis: Disability and the Dependencies of Discourse*. Ann Arbor: University of Michigan Press, 2000.

Mitchell, David T., and Snyder, L. Sharon. 'Re-engaging the Body: Disability Studies and the Resistance to Embodiment'. *Public Culture* 13 (2001): 367–89.

Shapiro, Joseph P. *No Pity. People with Disabilities Forging a New Civil Rights Movement*. New York: Three Rivers Press, 1993.

Sizeranne, Maurice de la. *The Blind as Seen through Blind Eyes*. Trans. F. Park Lewis. New York: M.D., 1893.

Stiker, Henri-Jaques. *A History of Disability*. Trans. William Sayers. Ann Arbor: University of Michigan Press, 1999.

Thomson, Rosemarie Garland. *Staring: How We Look*. New York: Oxford University Press, 2009.

Thomson, Rosemarie Garland. *Extraordinary Bodies. Figuring Physical Disability in American Culture and Literature*. New York: Columbia University Press, 1997.

Thurer, Shari. 'Disability and Monstrosity: A Look at Literary Distortions of Handicapping Conditions'. *Rehabilitation Literature* 41(1–2) (1980): 12–15.

Tunstall, Kate E. *Blindness and The Enlightenment: An Essay, with a New Translation of Diderot's* Essay on the Blind, *1749*. London: Continuum, 2011.

Zupancic, Alenka. 'Philosophers' Blind Man's Buff', in Renata Salecl and Slavoj Žižek (eds), *Gaze and Voice as Love Objects*. Durham, NC: Duke University Press, 1996.

Historical sources and commentary

Ackerman, Diane. *A Natural History of the Senses*. New York: Random House, 1990.

Ainlay, Stephen, Gaylene Becker and Lerita M. Coleman, eds. *The Dilemma of Difference: A Multidisciplinary View of Stigma*. New York: Plenum Press, 1986.

American Federation of the Blind. 'Helen Keller: A Love Affair'. 21 August 2016. Available online via afb.org.

Anagnos, Michael. *Education of the Blind*. Boston, 1882.

Anagnos, Michael. *'Workshops for the Blind': Proceedings of the Ninth Biennial Meeting of the American Association of Instructors of the Blind.* New York, 1886.

Barasch, Frances K. 'Introduction', in Thomas Wright, *A History of Caricature and Grotesque in Literature and Art*. New York: Frederick Ungar, 1968 (1865).

Bartley, G. C. *The Schools for the People containing the History, Development of English School for the Industrial and Poorer Classes*. London, 1871.

Bates, A. W. 'Dr Kahn's Museum: Obscene Anatomy in Victorian London'. *Journal of the Royal Society of Medicine* 99(12) (December 2006): 618–24.

Bird, John (ed.). 'Autobiography of the Blind James Wilson, Author of "The Lives of Useful Blind"; with Johns B. G. "The Blind". A Preliminary Essay on his Life, Character'. *Edinburgh Review*, 1854.

Bogdan, Robert. *Freak Show: Presenting Human Oddities for Fun and Profit*. Chicago: University of Chicago Press, 1988.

Braille, Louis. *Method of Writing Words, Music and Plain Songs by Means of Dots, for Use by the Blind and Arranged for them*. 1829.

Brontë, Charlotte. *Jane Eyre*. London: Norton Critical Edition, 1988.

Brown, Gillian. *Domestic Individualism: Imagining Self in Nineteenth Century America*. Berkeley: University of California Press, 1990.

Browne, Frances. *My Share of the World: An Autobiography*. General Books LLC, 2012 (1861).

Browne, Frances. 'The Life and Writings of Miss Browne, the Blind Poetess'. *Dublin Review* 34 (December 1844): 517–60.

Castleton, David. *In the Mind's Eye: The Blinded Veterans of St Dunstan's*. Barnsley, UK: Pen & Sword Military, 2013.

Cheselden, William. 'An account of some observations made by a young gentleman, who was born blind, or lost his sight so early, that he had no remembrance of ever having seen, and was couch'd between 13 and 14 years of age'. *Philosophical Transactions* 35 (1727–8).

Collins, Wilkie. *Poor Miss Finch*. Ed. Catherine Peters. Oxford: Oxford University Press, 2000 (1892).

Compton, Tom. *The Brief History of Disability*. Berkeley, CA: unpublished manuscript, 1989.

Craton, Lillian. *The Victorian Freak Show: The significance of disability and physical differences in 19th-century fiction*. Amherst, NY: Cambria Press, 2009.

Crubézy, Eric, and Trinkaus, Erik. 'Shanidar 1: A case of hyperostotic disease (DISH) in the middle paleolithic'. *American Journal of Physical Anthropology* 89(4) (December 1992): 411–20. doi:10.1002/ajpa.1330890402. PMID 1463085.

Danek, Adrian. '"On mind-blindness (optic agnosia)": a classical clinic-pathological report, and its author Wilhelm von Stauffenberg (1879–1918)'. *Journal of the History of the Neurosciences: Basic and Clinical Perspectives* 5(2) (1996): 126–35.

Dickens, Charles. *David Copperfield*. Ed. Jeremy Tambling. London: Penguin, 2004 (1849–50).

Dickens, Charles. *The Cricket on the Hearth. A Fairy Tale of Home*. Bradbury & Evans, 1845.

Dickens, Charles. *American Notes for General Circulation*. Chapman and Hall, 1842.

Encyclopaedia Britannica 1775. Blindness entry written by Dr Thomas Blacklock – 1st edn. Cambridge University Library.

Euripides. *Hecuba*. Trans. E. P. Coleridge. Revised by Casey Dué and Mary Ebbott. Based on the Greek text as edited by James Diggle. Oxford, 1994.

Felluga, Dino, Gilbert, Pamela, and Hughes, Linda (eds). 'Blind Authors and Blind Readers', in *Blackwell Encyclopaedia of Victorian Literature*. Oxford: Blackwell 2015.

Flower, Attyah Michael. *The Seer in Ancient Greece*. University of California Press, 2009.

French, Kimberley. *Perkins School for the Blind*. Charleston, SC: Arcadia Publishing, 2004.

Gerber, David. 'Volition and Valorization: The "Careers" of People Exhibited in Freak Shows', in Rosemarie Garland Thomson (ed.), *Freakery: Cultural Spectacles of the Extraordinary Body*. New York: New York University Press, 1996.

Goldstein, E. Bruce. *Sensation and Perception*. 3rd edn. Belmont, CA: Wadsworth, 1989.

Green, Henry. *Nothing, Doting, Blindness*. New York: Penguin, 1926.

Gridley Howe, Samuel. 'Education of the Blind'. *North American Review* 37(16) (1883).

Herndl, Diane Price. *Invalid Women: Figuring Illness in American Fiction and Culture, 1840–1940*. Chapel Hill: University of North Carolina Press, 1993.

Hillyer, Barbara. *Feminism and Disability*. Norman, OK: University of Oklahoma Press, 1993.

Hine, Robert V. *Second Sight*. Berkeley: University of California Press, 1993.

Homans, Margaret. *Bearing the Word: Language and Female Experience in Nineteenth-Century Women's Writing*. Chicago: University of Chicago Press, 1986.

Homer. *The Odyssey*, Book VIII. Trans. G. S. Kirk. Oxford University Press, 2008.

Illingworth, W. H. *History of the Education of the Blind*. London, 1910.

Ireson, Peter. *Another Pair of Eyes: The Story of Guide Dogs in Britain*. London: Pelham Books, 1991.

Katz, Michael B. *In the Shadows of the Poorhouse: A Social History of Welfare in America*. New York: Basic Books, 1986.

Kent, Deborah. 'In Search of a Heroine: Images of Women with Disabilities in Fiction and Drama', in Adrienne Asch and Michelle Fine (eds), *Women with Disabilities*. Philadelphia, PA: Temple University Press, 1988, pp. 90–110.

Kitto, John. *The Lost Senses: Deafness and Blindness*. 2 vols. Edinburgh: William Oliphant & Co., 1845.

Koestler, Frances A. *The Unseen Minority: A Social History of Blindness in the United States*. New York: David McKay, 1976.

Kondellas, B. 'The Educational Philosophy of Michael Anagnostopoulos, 1837–1906: Reflections on Universal Education'. Unpublished dissertation, 2001.

Kudlick, J. Catherine. *Guy de Maupassant, Louisa May Alcott and Youth at Risk: Lessons from the new paradigm of disability*. University of California, Davis, USA, 2009.

Kuusisto, Stephen. *Planet of the Blind*. London: Faber and Faber, 2002.

Lamb, Charles. *'A Complaint of the Decay of Beggars in the Metropolis': Essays of Elia and Last Essays of Elia*. London: J. M. Dent, 1972.

Larrissy, Edward. *The Blind and Blindness in the Literature of the Romantic Period*. Edinburgh: Edinburgh University Press, 2007.

Lawrence, D. H. 'The Blind Man', in *The Complete Short Stories*, vol. 2. London: William Heinemann, 1955.

Lawson, Arnold. *War Blindness at St Dunstan's*. Henry Frowde, 1922.

Lazerson, Marvin. 'The Origins of Special Education', in J. G. Chambers and William T. Hartman (eds), *Special Education Politics: Their History, Implementation, and Finance*. Philadelphia: Temple University Press, 1983.

Lees, Colin, and Ralph, Sue. 'Charitable provision for blind people and deaf people in late 19th-century London'. *Journal of Research in Special Educational Needs* 4(3) (2004): 148–60.

Lenihan, John. 'Disabled Americans: A History'. *Performance* (former magazine of The President's Committee on Employment of the Handicapped), November–December 1976/January 1977.

Malthus, Reverend T. R. *An Essay on the Principle of Population*. London: J. Johnson, in St Paul's Churchyard, 1798.

March, Jenny. *The Penguin Book of Classical Myths*. Penguin, 2008.

Martin, Frances. *Elizabeth Gilbert and her Work for the Blind*. New York: Macmillan, 1923.

Maxwell, Catherine. *The Female Sublime from Milton to Swinburne: Bearing Blindness*. Manchester University Press, 2001.

Maxwell, Catherine. *Second Sight: The Visionary Imagination in Late Victorian Literature*. Manchester University Press, 2008.

Mayhew, Henry. 'Clearing the Streets: Blindness and Begging. London Labour and the London Poor', in *City Limits: Perspectives on the Historical European City*. Montreal: McGill-Queen's University Press, 2010, pp. 205–26.

Mesmer, Franz Anton. *Mesmerism – A translation of the original medical and scientific writings of F. A. Mesmer*. Compiled and translated by George J. Block. William Kaufman, 1980.

Metzler, Irina. *Disability in Medieval Europe: Thinking about Physical Impairment in the High Middle Ages, c.1100–c.1400*. New York: Routledge, 2005.

Miller, Brian R. 'Speaking for themselves: The blind civil rights movement and the battle for the Iowa Braille School'. *Iowa Research Online* (2013): 1–479.

Milton, John. 'Sonnet 19 – On His Blindness.' Available online via Poetry Foundation.

Paulson, William. *Enlightenment, Romanticism, and the Blind in France*. Princeton, NJ: Princeton University Press, 1987.

Pearson, Sir Arthur. *Victory Over Blindness*. New York, 1919.

Phillips, Gordon. *The Blind in British Society: Charity, State and Community 1780 to 1900*. Aldershot: Ashgate, 2004.

Pope, Jaclyn. 'Why Assistive Technology Matters to Me: Jaclyn Pope – AdaptiVision'. 22 March 2022. Available online via lowvisionsource.com.

Porter, Roy. *Disease, Medicine, and Society in England, 1550–1860*. Cambridge University Press, 1993 (1987).

Porter, Roy (ed.). *Eighteenth-Century Science*. The Cambridge History of Science, vol. 4. Cambridge University Press, 2003.

Porter, Roy. *Flesh in the Age of Reason*. London: Penguin, 2005.

Rose, Martha. *The Staff of Oedipus: Transforming Disability in Ancient Greece*. Ann Arbor, MI: University of Michigan Press, 2003.

Rothman, David J. *The Discovery of the Asylum: Social Order and Disorder in the New Republic*. Rev. edn. Boston: Little, Brown and Company, 1990.

Royden, W. Michael. *Pioneers and Perseverance: A History of the Royal School for the Blind, Liverpool, 1791-1991*. Liverpool: Countyvise Ltd, 1991.

Sacks, Oliver. 'To see and not see'. *The New Yorker*, May 1993.

Saramago, José. *Blindness*. Trans. Giovanni Pontiero. Glasgow: The Harvill Press, 1999.

Scotch, Richard K. *From Good Will to Civil Rights: Transforming Federal Disability Policy*. Philadelphia: Temple University Press, 1984.

Scott, Robert A. *The Making of Blind Men: A Study of Adult Socialization*. New Brunswick, NJ: Transaction, 1969.

Smiles, Samuel. *Self-help*. Ed. Peter W. Sinnema. Oxford University Press, 2008.

Smith, Terry. Introduction to Jacques Derrida's 'In Blind Sight: Writing, Seeing, Touching', in Paul Patton and Terry Smith (eds), *Deconstruction Engaged: The Sydney Seminars*. Sydney: Power Publications, 2000, pp. 13-29.

Sophocles. *The Oedipus Cycle*. English version by Dudley Fitts and Robert Fitzgerald. Harcourt Brace Jovanovitch, 1977 (1939).

Sterrenberg, Lee. 'Mary Shelley's Monster: Politics and Psyche in *Frankenstein*', in George Levine and U. C. Knoepflmacher (eds), *The Endurance of Frankenstein: Essays on Mary Shelley's Novel*. Berkeley: University of California Press, 1979, pp. 143-71.

Symons, Arthur. 'The Blind Beggar' [1892], in *Poems by Arthur Symons*, vol. 1. London: Heinemann, 1927.

Thomas, Mary G. *The Royal National Institute for the Blind 1868-1956*. Royal National Institute for the Blind, 1957.

Thompson, Hannah. *Reviewing Blindness in French Fiction, 1789-2013*. Basingstoke: Palgrave Macmillan, 2013.

Tilley, Heather. 'Frances Browne, the "Blind Poetess": Towards a Poetics of Blind Writing'. *Journal of Literary and Cultural Disability Studies* 3(2) (July 2009): 147–61.

Valvo, Alberto. *Sight Restoration after Long-term Blindness*. American Foundation for the Blind, 1971.

Van Landeghem, Hippolyte. *Exile and Home: The Advantages of Social Education for the Blind*. London, 1865.

Van Landeghem, Hippolyte. 'Charity Misapplied. When Restored to Society after having been immured for several years in exile schools … the blind and the deaf and the dumb are found to be incapable of self-support'. London: Privately published, 1864.

Wagg, Henry T. *A Chronological Survey of Work for the Blind*. Sir Issac Pitman & Sons, 1932.

Warne, Vanessa. '"To Invest a Cripple with Peculiar Interest": Money, Mobility and Prosthetics at Mid-Century'. *Victorian Review* 35(2) (Fall 2009): 83–100.

Warne, Vanessa. 'How a Blind Man Saw the International Exhibition'. Lecture, Temple Bar, 1862.

Waxman, Olivia B. 'Co-Founding the ACLU, Fighting for Labor Rights and Other Helen Keller Accomplishments Students Don't Learn in School'. *Time*, 15 December 2020. https://time.com/5918660/helen-keller-disability-history/

Wells, H. G. 'The Country of the Blind', in *The Country of the Blind and Other Stories*. Ed. Michael Sherborne. Oxford University Press, 1996.

Weygand, Zina. *The Blind in French Society: From the Middle Ages to the Century of Louis Braille*. Stanford University Press, 2009.

Weygand, Zina, and Kudlick, Catherine. *Reflections: The Life and Writings of a Young Woman in Post-revolutionary France*. NYU Press, 2002.

Wheatley, Edward. *Stumbling Blocks before the Blind: Medieval Constructions of Disability*. Ann Arbor, MI: University of Michigan Press, 2010.

Wilde, Oscar, 'Essays on Aesthetics'. Available online: (https://listentogenius.com/author.php/171.

Wilson, James. *Biography of the Blind, Including the Lives of All Those, from Homer down to the Present Day, who have Distinguished themselves, as Poets, Philosophers, Artists etc.* Belfast: Lyons, 1821.

Wilson, James. *'The Lives of Useful Blind'; with a Preliminary Essay on his Life, Character, and Writings, As Well as on the Present State of the Blind.* London: Ward & Lock, 1856.

Wyndham, John. *The Day of the Triffids.* London: Michael Joseph, 1951.

Youngquist, Paul. *Monstrosities: Bodies and British Romanticism.* Minneapolis: University of Minnesota Press, 2003.

INDEX

ableism, 115
abuse, 248
acceptance, 219
accessible tech, 16
acute visual fatigue, 131
adaptation, 110
advantages, 235–7, 248
adversity, triumph over, 8–9
advertising, 42
Aeschylus, 27
agency, 86–7
aids and adaptations, 214–18, 241–2, 248
   apps, 238
   audio description, 235–7
   canes and cane training, 216–18
   consent, 241–2
   guide dogs, 228–35
   questioning, 238–41
   reading systems, 220–8
   speech to text technology, 239
   voiceovers and audio tech, 228
Alcott, Louisa May, 187–8
Al-Kindi, 118, 119
amavrophelia, 7
ambiguity, 15
Ambrose, St, 57
American Foundation for the Blind (AFB), 88
anger, 80–1
anglerfish, 76–7
animal magnetism, 136
Anna (adaptations specialist), 215–18
Antichrist, the, 93, 94
Apartheid, 205
apps, 238
Aristophanes, 39–40
Aristotle, 28, 45
Armitage, Thomas Rhodes, 171, 227
artistic representations, 9, 101–2
Athena, 34
audio description, 235–7
audio tech, 228
autobiography, 25–6

Bach, Johann Sebastian, 126
Baghdad, 118
baptism, 67
Baudelaire, Charles, 191–2
BBC Radio, 79
Berkeley, Bishop George, 123
Berlin, 231
bias, 247
Bible, the, 54, 57–8, 93
   Acts of the Apostles, 69–70
   and blame, 65–6
   Gospel of St John, 65–6, 68
   Gospel of St Mark, 66
   Gospel of St Matthew, 100–1
   New Testament references, 56, 64–73, 77

Bibliotequa Apostolica Vaticana (Vatican library), 60–2
Bird, John, 171
Birrer, Jakob, 230
Blacklock, Thomas, 158–9, 160, 235
blame, 65–6
blind, the, 20
blind beggars, 96–7, 99–102
blind inspirational innocent, the, 187–93
blind life, assumptions about, 49–50
blind people
  definition, 15
  perception of, 2
blind voices, 26–7, 160, 164–8, 178, 246
  social media, 246
blindfolds, 55–6
blindness
  adjusting to, 5
  causes, 17n
  change in perspective, 246–50
  closing reflections, 243–50
  concept of, 12
  describing, 6
  fantasies about, 7, 13
  fascination of, 249
  fear of, 249
  interpretation of, 12
  legal definition, 2
  perception of, 2
  presumptions of, 23–6
  sighted views of, 10
  spectrum of, 6
'Blindness and Dreams' lecture, 203–9
blindness rates, 4
blue goo process, 84
Blue Peter, 229
Blunkett, David, 23–4
Borges, Jorge Luis, 33
Braille, 25, 192, 223–4, 227–8
Braille, Louis, 9, 223–4
Bridgeman, Laura, 189–90
Brighton, 225
British Library, 24, 26, 46–7
British Museum, 43–4
Brontë, Charlotte, 193–6
Brueghel the Elder, 101
burden, 180–3
bureaucracy, 214

Callimachus, 34
canes and cane training, 216–18
Cardano, Geronimo, 220
cataract surgery, 107, 108–9, 112, 115
cathedrals, 55–6
Cecilia, St, 75
charity, 91, 156
charity adverts, 42
Charity model, 76
Chartres Cathedral, 55
Cheselden, William, 123–6, 128
Chevalier, John, 126
choice, 197–8, 200–1
Christianity, 50, 55–7, 64–76
Clarity, 172
classical era, 90
clumsiness, 3
Cockney, 16
Codex of Rossano, 67–73

INDEX

collective identity, 171, 182
Collins, Wilkie, 187–8
   Poor Miss Finch, 196–8
colour, 206–7
   missing, 16
confidence, 154
consent, 241–2
Constantine, Emperor, 72
couching, 117
courage, 73, 185, 249
creation myths, 52, 54
creativity, 36
cruelty, 99
cures, 113–16
   ancient practices, 116–20
   consent, 241–2
   eighteenth century, 120–8
   fraudulent, 125–7
   gene therapy, 114
   insistence on, 116
   media focus on, 113–15
   morality of, 113
   rebellion against, 133–8
   regret at taking, 128–33
Cyclopes, the, 38–9

daily struggle, 219–20
Daily Telegraph, 2, 19, 79, 107–10
Dante Alighieri, 5
Dare Devil, 41
darkness, 78
   and death, 52
   definition, 53
   and ignorance, 62, 75–6
   and light, 51–7
   positive use, 53
dating, 85–7

Daviel, Jacques, 124
Davis, Leonard, 193
De Quincey, Thomas, 173
deaf community, 171
deafness, 45
DeGeneres, Ellen, 102–4
denial, 152
depression, 130–1
Descartes, René, 119
Devil, the, 93–4
Dickens, Charles, 182, 187–8, 192, 196
   blind characters, 190–1
   visit to America, 188–90
Diderot, Denis, 121
   Lettre sur les aveugles à l'usage de ceux qui voient, 86–7
Didymus, 220
Diocletian, Emperor, 73
disability, understanding, 92–3
disability history, 14
divination, 30
Diwali, 52
dreams, 202–9
driving, 151–2
Dyckmans, Josephus Laurentius, 102

Ecclesia, 55
Edinburgh, 169, 224–5, 226
education
   access, 157, 163
   author's parents' view on disability, 147–55
   battles, 148–50
   blind advocates, 170–8
   blind voices, 164–8
   and choice, 183–5

historical background, 155–83
industrial training, 169–70
Iowa Blind and Sight Saving School visit, 141–6
low expectations, 150
normality philosophy, 146–55
participation, 146–55
primary school, 148–9
Edward II, King of England, 35
Egyptians, ancient, 52
Eliot, T. S., 33
The Waste Land, 32–3
Ellen (TV show), 102–4
emotional trauma, 13
empathy, 19
engagement, terms of, 63
entertainment, blind people as, 95–9, 102–5, 161–2
Euenius, 30
Euripides, 39–40
Eustis, Dorothy Harrison, 231–2
Everest, 9, 41
evil associations, 89–95
evil fantasies, 95
exclusion, 78
ex-servicemen, 230–1
eyes, treatment of, 44–5
eyesight stories, strangers sharing, 111–12

Fagan, Peter, 205
Fagnani, Doctor Prospero, 60–2, 63
faith, 67–76
faking it, 85, 89, 101–2, 244
accusations of, 79–81
false eyes, 19–20, 80–1, 89
blue goo process, 84

cleaning, 84
daytime, 84
fitting, 81–5
manufacture, 83–4
nighttime, 84
party, 84
replacement, 85
fantasies, about blindness, 7, 13
Farrell, Gabriel, 10
fictional representations, 7–8, 187–202, 209–11, 211
the blind inspirational innocent, 187–93
liberating, 196–9
as narrative device, 188
and redemption, 193–6
science fiction, 199–202
First World War, 57
fish, 76–7
fitting in, 85, 89
Foster, Father Reginald, 58–64, 76
France, 156, 164–6, 191–2
Institut des Jeunes Aveugles, 161–3
freedom, 151
Freke, John, 124
French farce, 98–9

Galen of Pergamon, 45, 117
Gall, James, 224–5
Garfunkel, Art, 17
gene therapy, 114
General Welfare Association, 172–8
Gilbert, Elizabeth, 172–8
Girma, Haben, 210
Gladstone, William, 168, 172, 176

God, light of, 77
Goffman, Erving, 90
good and evil, 54
Grant, Roger, 128
Great Exhibition, 1851, 226
Greece, Ancient, 27–30
Greek tragedy, 37–8, 39–40
Greenberg, Sandy, 18
Guardian, 23
guide dogs, 228–35
Guide Dogs for the Blind Association, 232
Guild of the Brave Poor Things, 177

Hanukkah, 53
Haüy, Valentin, 134–8, 161–3, 221–3
Hecuba, Queen of Troy, 39–40
'Hello Darkness, My Old Friend' (Simon and Garfunkel), 17
helplessness, 195
Hera, 34
Herodotus, 28, 30, 45
hero-worshipping attitudes, 24–6
Hesiod, 34
Hilmer, Joseph, 126–7
historians, 23, 26–7
historical achievers, 24–5
historical context, 8–9
Homer, 8, 27–30, 31–2, 34
hopelessness, 191–2
Howe, Gridley, 169, 226
human nature, 26–7
humiliation, 99, 248
Husson, Thérèse-Adèle, 164–7, 191
Huxley, Aldous, 9

idealism, 166
identity, 76
Iditarod sled trail, 9
ignorance, 55–6, 62, 71, 75–6, 148
In The Dark (TV series), 42
independence, 147, 204, 228, 245
Industrial Revolution, 180, 187
industrial training, 169–70
Ingalls, Mary, 142, 145, 155
Institut des Jeunes Aveugles, 161–3
intelligence, 45
interior life, 87
Iowa Blind and Sight Saving School, 141–6, 169
isolation, 153, 210

Jane Eyre, 193–6
Jefferson, Thomas, 121
Jerome, St, 57
Jesus, 65–7, 68, 71, 77, 100–1
Johnson, Lyndon, 85
Jones, William, 128

Kant, Immanuel, 120–1
Keller, Helen, 9, 189, 199, 203–9, 210
    dreams, 206–8
    left-wing socialist views, 205
    love match thwarted, 205–6
    prejudices, 204
    social media debate, 87–8
Kendall, Adam, 142
Kleege, Georgina, 33
Klein, Johann Wilhelm, 230
knowledge, 58–9
Kudlick, Cathy, 165, 166

language, 15
languages, study of, 58–9
Latin, 90
Le Garcon et l'Aveugle, 96–7
legal blindness, 213–14
Lendegem, Hippolyte van, 167
Leonardo Da Vinci, 118
Levy, William Hank, 174–7
light, 118–19
  benefits of, 53–4
  creation of, 54
  and darkness, 51–7
  emergence of, 52–3
  and truth, 52
limits, 154
Little House on the Prairie (TV series), 142
Liverpool, School for the Indigent Blind, 168
Locke, John, 125
  An Essay on Human Understanding, 121–3
loneliness, presumption of, 42
Lord, Albert, 29
loss, 61
Lucas, Francesco, 220–1
Lucy of Syracuse, St, 72–3

Maccabees, 53
Malthusian theory, 177
Margaret of Metola, St, 75
Matrix, The (film), 41
Maupassant, Guy de, 187–8
medical treatment, 44–5
Mehta, Ved, 9
memoirs, 9
mental agility testing, 149
Mesmer, Franz Anton, 135–8

Metzler, Irene, 92
Middle Ages, 35
  anxiety, 99
  blind beggars, 96–7, 99–102
  blind people as entertainment, 95–9
  evil status of blindness, 89–95
  social hierarchies, 90–1
  understanding of disability, 92–3
Middle English, 15, 89–90
Millais, John Everett, 102
Miller, Brian, 141
Mills, Selina, 214–18
  acceptance, 219
  accused of fakery, 79–81
  aids and adaptations, 215–20
  'Blindness and Dreams' lecture, 203–9
  cane training, 216–18
  career, 79
  change in perspective, 246–50
  closing reflections, 243–50
  cut cornea, 107–10
  daily struggle, 219–20
  dating, 85–7
  denial, 79
  deterioration, 110–11
  education, 147–55
  extent of vision, 6, 14–15, 80, 116
  eye colour, 82–3
  eyesight problems, 3
  false eye, 19–20, 80–1, 81–5, 89
  first lesson, 47
  husband, 16
  husband courts, 86–7
  independence, 147
  Iowa Blind and Sight Saving School visit, 141–6

learns to drive, 151–2
learns to ski, 151
legally blind diagnosis, 213–14
loss of sight, 3–8, 11, 16
Mobility Team visit, 214
odyssey, 46–7
overdraft interview, 19–20
parents' view on disability, 147–55, 185
post-anterior cataract, 4, 107, 111
relationship to blindness, 104
self definition, 46
visits specialists, 110–11
Milton, John, 'On his Blindness', 30–1
mind, loss of, 57
miracle stories, 67–73, 92
Miracle Worker, The (film), 87
missionaries, 168, 225
Mitchell, Alexander, 171
mobility, 166
Molyneux, William, 122
    Molyneux question, 122, 125
Moon, William, 225
Moorfields Eye Hospital, 108–9
moral smugness, 246–7
Moses, 54
Murillo, Sandy, 228
musical talent, 134–8

Nandy (Neanderthal), 19, 21–3, 47, 76, 246
National Geographic, 113–14, 116
National League of the Blind, 171
Navajo, the, 52–3
Neanderthals, 19, 20–3, 47

negative connotations, 90
New England Asylum for the Blind *see* Perkins Institute for the Blind
New Yorker, 130–1
Newton, Sir Isaac, 119
non-seeing, 33, 78
Norse language, 15
Notre Dame Cathedral, 55

objectification, 105
Observer, 128
occuphelia, 7
ocularcentrism, 15
Odile of Alsace, St, 73–6
Odin, 35
Odysseus, 38–9
Odyssey, The (Homer), 28
Oedipus, 37–8, 195
othering, 10
otherness, 25–6, 188, 191–3, 198–9, 199–201, 209–11, 247
ownership, 64–5

Paradis, Maria Theresia von, 134–40, 206
Paradis Files, The (opera), 139, 206
Paralympics, 42
parents, dilemma facing, 147–55
Paris, 98, 229
    Institut des Jeunes Aveugles, 161–3
Parry, Milman, 29
Parthenon Marbles, 43
participation, 147–55
paternalism, 144
patience, 80
Paul, St, 56, 69–70, 77, 93, 195

Paula (eye maker), 82–4
perception
  new information changing, 22
  of treatment, 26
Pergamon Museum, Berlin, 29
Perkins Institute for the Blind, 169, 189, 226
Philanthropic Society of Paris, 162
philanthropy, 156, 170, 182–3
physical theatre, 103–4
pity, 49–52, 71, 76, 78, 195, 210, 219
  overcoming, 57–64
Plutarch, 45
Polyphemus, the Cyclopes, 38–9
Poor Laws, 180–2
post-anterior cataracts, 4, 107, 111
poverty, 180–3
prayer, 67
prejudice, 147–8
psychological trauma, 13
punishment, blindness as, 35, 37–40, 41, 54, 91–5

reading, 25, 220–8
redemption, 193–6
Renaissance, the, 30
Roman eye-votives, 44
Rome, 49–52, 57–64
  Bibliotequa Apostolica Vaticana (Vatican library), 60–2
  Sistine Chapel, 59–60, 63
  Venerable English College, 51
Rome, ancient, 229
Roosevelt, Franklin D., 85
Rose, Martha, 44–5

Royal Blind Pension Society of the United Kingdom, 157
Royal National Institute of Blind People, 171
Royal Society, 124
Rushton, Edward, 168

Sacks, Oliver, 130–1, 132
sacrifice, 35
Said, Edward, 211
St John's Wood School for the Blind, 176
Saramago, José, 199, 202
Saul, 16
Scdoris, Rachael, 9
School for the Indigent Blind, Liverpool, 168
science fiction, 199–202
self-definition, 13, 46
self-determination, 155
self-improvement, 169–70
self-referencing community, 144
self-reliance, fantasy of, 239
self-sufficiency, 156, 158–9, 169–70, 175–6, 177, 178, 192
Senden, Marius Von, 131–2
senses, enhanced, 7, 23, 207, 248
Sesotris, Egyptian pharaoh, 45
Shanidar 1 (Nandy (Neanderthal)), 19–20, 21–3
shellshock, 57
sight, loss of, 3–8, 11, 16
sight impairment, spectrum of, 6
Simon, Paul, 17
sin, 91–5
Sistine Chapel, Rome, 59–60, 63
skiing, 151

smartphones, 238
Smiles, Samuel, 159
Smith, John Thomas, 101
Snellius, Willebrord, 119
social hierarchies, 90–1
social isolation, 210
social justice, 205
social media, 244–5
    Helen Keller debate, 87–8
Sodom and Gomorrah, 54
software, 16
Sophocles, *Oedipus Rex*, 37–8
South London Association for Assisting the Blind, 159
specialness, 13
Spectator, 128
spectrum, of blindness, 6
speech to text technology, 239
spiritual health, 67
spirituality, 62
stained-glass images, 55–6
Stalling, Gerhard, 230
stigma and stigmatization, 78, 89–95, 100, 105, 153, 209
stimulus, lack of, 167
Sullivan, Annie, 87–8, 205
sun, the, 52
superheroes, 41
superstitions, 94
surgery, caveats, 111
survival mechanisms, 11
sympathy, 115
Synagoga, 55–6

Tacitus, Gaius Cornelius, 68
talent, and blindness, 28, 31–2, 33, 36, 134–40
Tatler, 128

teachers, battles with, 148–50
teachers, blind, 142
technological fix, questioning, 238–41
television, 42
temperament, 129
Tenberken, Sabriye, 210
Tertullian, 67
Testament of the Lord, 94
theologians, 56–7
Thucydides, 28
The Times, 139
Tiresias, 32–3, 34–5, 37–8, 65
tragedy, 13
trance states, 29
transformation, 69–70
Trevor-Roper, Patrick, 129
Trismegistus, Hermes, 77
truth, inner, 73
Twitter, 42, 244–5

United States of America
    blindness rate, 4–5
    Dickens visits, 188–90
    reading systems, 226–7

vanity, 166
Venerable English College, Rome, 51
Vespasian, 68
Victoria, Queen, 172, 175, 176, 189
Victorian values, 159
Vienna, 126, 134–8, 230
Virgil, 5, 39–40
Virgil (sight-restoree), 130
visual memory, 130
vocabulary, 15–16

voice, 26–7, 160–1, 164–8, 178, 246
  social media, 246
voiceovers, 228
Voltaire, 121
votives, 44
voyeurism, 210

Wallen, Errollyn, 138–9
Weihenmayer, Erik, 9
Wells, H. G. 199–201
Weygand, Zina, 161, 165, 166
Wheatley, Edward, 92, 98

Wilde, Oscar, 31–2, 33
Wilson, James, 164
wisdom, and blindness, 35
Wordsworth, William, 173
workhouses, 181–2
World Health Organization, 4, 115
writing, 25
Wyndham, John, 199, 201–2

Zagros Mountains, 21
Zeus, 30, 34
Zorn, Trischa, 210